# Wisconsin's Historic Courthouses

**Photos by L. Roger Turner**
**Text by Marv Balousek**

Badger Books Inc.
P.O. Box 192
Oregon, WI 53575

**ISBN 1-878569-56-2**

*For Yvonne and Barbara*

Wisconsin's historic courthouses have been rightfully called "Temples of Justice." They are dedicated to preserving the promises and guarantees of liberty and self-government written into the United States and Wisconsin constitutions by "we, the people."

In 1818, while still a part of Michigan territory, Wisconsin was divided into three counties. As the population increased, further subdivisions into additional counties were made when Wisconsin became a territory in 1836 and a state in 1848.

From 1836 to 1901, the number of counties went from six to 71. In 1961, Menominee County was added, making our present total of 72.

The Wisconsin Revised Statutes of 1849, chapter 10, section 16, provided in part:

"Each county organized for judicial purposes shall, at its own expense, provide a suitable court house . . . and keep the same in good repair."

Today, section 59.54 (14) of the Wisconsin Statutes is strikingly similar.

The counties are often referred to as agents of the state because, by statute, many state laws are enforced and carried out by various elected county officials, frequently located in the courthouse. But the primary function in the courthouse is a judicial one, carried out by the circuit courts.

Our forebears in constructing our "Temples of Justice" sought to preserve and to remind us of our heritage — and our hopes.

*Roland B. Day*

This book illustrates the success of their worthy goals.

We are indebted to L. Roger Turner for the beautiful photographs his artistic skill has created and to Marv Balousek for his scholarly research on the history of the county courthouses in Wisconsin. These buildings are treasures of our heritage. This book is an excellent contribution to the celebration of Wisconsin's Sesquicentennial.

— **Roland B. Day**
**Chief Justice (Ret.)**
**Wisconsin Supreme Court**

Introduction

The county courthouse is the quintessential symbol of county government. It represents in bricks and mortar the essence of our democracy. The county courthouse also physically signifies the pride we have in county government as it administers the nation's unparalleled system of justice.

Together, Wisconsin's historic county courthouses tell a fascinating story that stretches from the founding of Wisconsin's earliest communities to the twentieth century urban revitalization of its larger cities. Their architectural significance often speaks for itself. In many cases the county courthouse is the most striking example of architecture for many miles in any direction. Its historical significance is not always as obvious, however, and an historian is generally needed to ferret out the full scope of a courthouse's impact on a community.

Origins of the county governmental system have their roots in Anglo-Saxon precedent. This system was and still is a powerful organizational principle that took deep root in how we as Americans settled the land. Although the concept of county government is English in its origins, the county courthouse and its associated "courthouse square" is an American invention. Under provisions of an 1824 act of Congress, county governments were allowed to preempt, at a minimum price, two quarter-sections (320 acres) of land for the establishment of a seat of justice. Settlers traversing the American West in their migration westward brought the precepts of this American icon with them.

In the former Taylor County Courthouse and Jail, situated on a small promontory overlooking the community of Medford, Wisconsin, the two buildings together represent an example of that classic pairing of a major and minor form — with the dominant larger courthouse coupled by proximity and style to the smaller and separate, but complementary, jail.

The first three counties in Wisconsin (Brown, Iowa and

## Rick Bernstein
### State Historical Society

**Foreword**

Crawford) were established in 1818 while still a part of the Michigan Territory. Subsequently, the new State of Wisconsin was empowered by Article IV of the Wisconsin Constitution to create and regulate counties. Counties were meant to serve as administrative sub-units of state government; being intermediaries between the state and municipalities. Counties have traditionally been charged with such responsibilities as the discharge of social services, the maintenance of a county road system, the establishment of a county sheriff's office and jail and the maintenance of a county courts system, which explains why 68 of Wisconsin's current 72 counties are coterminous in their boundaries with judicial circuits.

County courthouses were often the first public buildings that early settlers erected. Among other things, this reflected the hope communities had of serving as the county seat. This competitive spirit carried over into the construction of the courthouse, with each community trying to outdo the other in the creation of a fitting building. In some cases, however, land speculation and charlatanism were also factors.

The "floating courthouse" is a preeminent example. The Pierce brothers discovered that newly formed Buffalo County had located its courthouse in Section 1-19N-12W — which was right in the middle of a slough of the Mississippi River and not, as everyone had expected, in the village of Fountain City. The two brothers rushed to the site, which they happened to own, and "seized a stray lumber raft, clapped together a shack and called it a courthouse." They took it upon themselves to "notify Fountain City officials that the county offices must be moved to the new location ... on the plea that acts done elsewhere were illegal."

Lawyers supported their claim and the county did indeed move its offices and a new settlement arose called Upper Fountain City. The original Fountain City built a stately courthouse and offered it at a bargain to the county. In 1859 the offer was accepted and county offices were moved back to Fountain City. Two years later a special election was held and the county seat was moved yet again to Alma, where it remains today.

Completion of the Soo line to Amery, a new rail community sixteen miles east of Osceola, led to an intense rivalry. In 1889, the promoters of the nearby community of Amery presented the first of several petitions calling for

the removal of the county seat from Osceola. For the next seven years, a bitter struggle ensued. The question was ultimately decided in a countywide referendum in 1898, which located the county seat in Balsam Lake, a third neutral community, in large part because a county courthouse had not yet been constructed. The decision resulted in the building of a new courthouse. Had such an investment been made previous to the referendum it is quite possible that Osceola would have retained its title as county seat. The second Polk County Courthouse in Balsam Lake is also listed in the National Register and has served as the Polk County Museum since 1975.

A classic example of how investment in a substantial county facility can directly influence the development of a village is the construction of the Pepin County Courthouse and Jail. Built in 1873-4, they were central factors in the nineteenth century growth of the village of Durand and a pivotal element in the turbulent controversy surrounding the final selection of a county seat. Although there were disputes of a similar nature in other counties, the battle in Pepin County is notable for its duration — thirty years passed during which three villages variously served as the county seat. For a brief period (1881-6) the designation passed from Durand to the neighboring village of Arkansaw. By 1886, it became apparent that a new facility was needed to replace the temporary building in Arkansaw, which was considered inadequate for conducting business and for the safe storage of county records. The cost of new facilities, however, would mean the imposition of a tax to establish a building fund.

Durand boasted that the county could have the old courthouse back for $1, if, and only if, the county seat were returned to the village. As one local newspaper said: "This, in brief, is the situation. Let the county seat remain at Arkansaw and a heavy tax is necessary to erect new buildings. Move it to Durand, and no expenses will be incurred."

The question was put to the voters. The argument for economy won out, and the seat was permanently relocated to Durand. This building still stands and is occupied by the Pepin County Historical Society.

Not every county courthouse is a grand edifice. In some cases the earliest generation of county courthouses were rather humble, especially those built in the earliest years of American settlement. For instance there is the Geiger Building, or old Polk County Courthouse, in Osceola, built in 1874 and used as a courthouse from 1882-1899. The Geiger Building is listed on the National Register as the only surviving structure associated with county government during the forty-five years that Osceola was the county seat. For the 17 years Polk County leased the structure, the basement housed the county jail, the first level housed all county offices, and the third level contained apartments for the county sheriff and the judge. The building has housed a variety of commercial establishments since the turn of the century.

The mandate that county government shall be responsible for the maintenance of a county sheriff and a county jail system often results in unique physical forms. The Crawford County Courthouse is an enduring landmark closely associated with the political and governmental affairs of the region since 1867. The historic jail, situated in the basement of the west wing of the courthouse, is a rare surviving example of a mid-nineteenth century penal facility. Some say that the 1867 courthouse was built on the basement of its 1843 predecessor making this the oldest jail in the state, but these contentions have never been fully documented. Nonetheless, this enduring feature adds to the building's historical significance.

Like many county jails built during the late nineteenth century, the Romanesque Revival Clark County Jail, built in 1897, was completely separate from the main body of the courthouse. Often included within county jails was a residence for the county sheriff and his family, in this case the first few floors of the front part of the building. The sheriff's wife was usually responsible for the cooking, not only for her family, but for the prisoners as well. This type of penal facility no longer represents current theories about corrections, but it does speak eloquently about bygone concepts of penology.

The 1938 Juneau County Courthouse in Mauston reversed the nineteenth century trend toward separation by reuniting the jail and the main body of the courthouse. Like the Clark County Jail, it includes a residence for the sheriff and his family. In this case, however, the jail itself is found in the penthouse, supposedly a more secure part of the facility. Just as importantly, the Juneau County courthouse is a historically significant Works Projects Administration (WPA) project, whose construction employed local workers, rejuvenated a sagging economy, and strengthened the county government. Constructed during the final years of the Great Depression, the Juneau County Courthouse is the most important WPA structure in the county. No other WPA project in the county rivalled this one in terms of size, cost or continuing relevance to everyday life.

The location of a county courthouse within a community was also an important part of its history. In many cases, the plat for a new community reserved its most prominent location for a new county courthouse, in hopes of securing the honor and perhaps ensuring the community's viability as well. The choice of the building's site, was often chosen to literally heighten its prominence within the community.

The setting of a courthouse could also be augmented by the arrangement of the surrounding development. Buildings grouped around the courthouse could provide the structure with an inspiring distinction, a distinction often sought by early American town planners, but rarely realized. Built in 1891, the Green County courthouse in Monroe is not only one of the state's best examples of the Ro-

*Foreword*

manesque style, but the architectural centerpiece of the state's single most popular town square. The Green County courthouse's significance as an architectural gem is magnified by its placement at the center of a vibrant historic commercial district that surrounds the courthouse on all four sides. The courthouse square has often been considered the center of civic rural life. The biennial Cheese Days celebration in Monroe demonstrates how a setting such as this can provide an important venue for community events that in turn provide residents and visitors with a communal focal point not often found, but almost always highly valued.

In addition to being the centerpiece in new town planning, county courthouses could also be catalysts for the renovation of older established cities. Kenosha officials discussed a major renovation of the city as early as 1908. In 1922, voters approved the city manager form of government. The vote heralded a new era in city government and intergovernmental cooperation. Harland Bartholomew, a planner of national reputation, was hired by Kenosha to put his ideas down on paper. Bartholomew's proposals included beautiful renderings of a brand new Kenosha including a perspective drawing showing a new system of parks and grand boulevards. Bartholomew's Kenosha plan also included a proposal for a large civic center that would group various public institutions together. The architectural styling was based on the monumental grouping of buildings the world saw at the 1893 Chicago World's Fair. It took ten years, but Bartholomew's suggestions were finally implemented. Today, all four sides of a large open space are enclosed. Besides a courthouse, buildings include a federal post office, a high school and a public museum. By the time the Bartholomew plan was published in 1925, the first building of the civic center was just being dedicated — the county courthouse. As the cornerstone of the Kenosha Civic Center, the courthouse was recognized throughout the state as an example to small cities of how much can be accomplished. An outstanding, and inspiring example of the Beaux Arts, the Kenosha County Courthouse also has historical significance, representing an important accomplishment in the history of Kenosha's community planning and development. According to historian Nelson Peter Ross, the courthouse and the civic center which grew around it, "served as a crowning symbol of the new Kenosha," embodying the "progressive spirit of the city's leaders in the classic age of the manager system."

Each of Wisconsin's historic county courthouses has a unique story to tell. It's a story that is stoically preserved in marble and stone, but still vulnerable to fleeting changes in tastes and lack of appropriate care. Reading this book should encourage our appreciation for these silent stalwarts of history.

— **Rick Bernstein**
**State Historical Society**
**of Wisconsin**

Wisconsin's county courthouses provide historical testimony to the evolution of the legal system and county government in the state. A typical pattern was that wooden courthouses were hastily assembled during the early years of statehood. Later, county officials viewed the courthouse as the focal point of public life in their communities and symbols of justice as they sought fitting and more elaborate structures.

The lack of adequate heating and electrical systems as well as an emphasis on modernization doomed some of these historic buildings during the mid-twentieth century. In some cases, such as Douglas County, courthouses were modernized while meticulous care was taken to preserve the original structure. In recent years, more of the state's aging county courthouses have been threatened by modernization while others have been preserved.

Although this book has been a major project of ours, many others have contributed to its successful publication.

First, we want to thank all of the helpful courthouse employees throughout Wisconsin who provided vital information about these historic structures. They include Harold Reckelberg of Kewaunee County, Steve Steadman of La Crosse County, Paul Syverson of Trempealeau County, Don Phillips of Marinette County and, especially, Topf Wells of Dane County, who suggested the idea for this book.

Our research was greatly aided by the State Historical Society of Wisconsin and the Wisconsin Supreme Court. Both shared their files on Wisconsin courthouses. Thanks to Rick Bernstein, Jim Draeger and Tracy Will of the historical society and to Karen Leone de Nie, Trina Haag and Amanda Todd

of the Supreme Court staff. We appreciate Paul Kending and Beth Sorge also helping with our research.

We also were assisted by postcard collectors who generously shared their photos of historic courthouses. Ann Waidelich offered several photos and another was supplied by Wilfred Harris. Thanks also to Mary Bloedow of the Rusk County Public Library for supplying a historic photo of that county's courthouse.

Thanks to Bob and Joan Franzmann for serving as the photographer's helpers, to Rich Rygh for his imaging assistance, to Jim Devine of Port to Print and to Ellen Heath for her design suggestions and copyediting.

We also thank retired Chief Justice Roland Day for his encouragement, strong interest in Wisconsin history and willingness to contribute an introduction.

Most of all, we thank our wives, Yvonne and Barbara, for their support and understanding of the long hours involved in completing this project.

More than half of Wisconsin's courthouses are listed in the National Register of Historic Places. We have indicated the historic status for each existing courthouse. Unfortunately, some of the state's magnificent courthouses have been torn down.

We hope this book serves both as a sesquicentennial salute to Wisconsin's historic courthouses and as a valuable reference in future years to these important public structures.

— **L. Roger Turner**
**Marv Balousek**

# Wisconsin's Historic Courthouses

Adams County

The original Adams County courthouse was a two-story wooden structure at the existing courthouse site. The courthouse square was used for basketball, croquet and Civil War troops camped there on their way to Camp Randall in Madison. The building itself was a gathering spot for Friday-night ice cream socials.

The existing courthouse was completed in 1914. Although the county had architectural plans in 1912, voters did not approve the $30,000 bond issue until 1913. The vote was divided between rival communities Adams and Friendship. Adams voters opposed the bond issue 158-18 while Friendship voters favored it 127-4.

The Pinery Road through Adams County was a major trade route during the mid-1800s for lumberjacks, traders and settlers headed for the North Woods. Taverns and trading posts sprung up along the route.

By 1860, the county's population reached 6,000 as transplanted Easterners were attracted by the supply of white pine for building and heating homes. The next wave of immigrants came in the 1890s from Germany, Bohemia and Poland.

Friendship, the county seat, was incorporated in 1907 but the Chicago & North Western Railroad didn't arrive until three years later.

The 1914 courthouse is based on a Neoclassi-

**Adams County**

County seat: **Friendship**
**Current Courthouse**
  Year built: 1914
  Historic status: **Listed in the National Register of Historic Places.**

cal design, dominated by a central pavilion and a portico. The brick building is nearly cubic, rising from a raised basement to a pitched roof.

**Seating is plentiful inside an Adams County courtroom, above, while the courthouse in winter is on the opposite page.**

Adams County

# Ashland County

Ashland County was created in 1860 with land taken from Michlimackinac, Chippewa, St. Croix and La Pointe counties. The county was subdivided in 1892 into the current Ashland and Iron counties.

Ashland's first settlers were Asaph Whittlesey and George Kilbourne, who left La Pointe in July 1854 and built the first house on the city's western limits. Ashland first was known as Whittlesey but the city's name was changed in 1860 to honor Henry Clay, who lived in Ashland, Kentucky.

The first courthouse, a two-story frame building of Italianate-Neoclassical design, was built on

**Ashland County**

County seat: Ashland
Current Courthouse
Year built: 1915
Historic status: Listed in the National Register of Historic Places.

A grandfather-style clock is in a courthouse hallway, at right, while a long view of a courtroom is above. An exterior view is on the opposite page.

the site now occupied by the Ashland Post Office.

The current Ashland County courthouse, a three-story ashlar-veneer building with a large colonnade, was built in 1915 at a cost of $134,363. A limestone parapet trims a low truncated hip roof. The roof follows the contours of project-ing corner pavilions and anthemions mark the corners.

Ashland County has sixty-four lakes which cover 11,000 acres. It also is the home of a great divide, where waters flow north to Lake Superior and south to the Mississippi River.

**Barron County**

A bitter battle between Barron and Rice Lake over which would be the county seat dominated the early years of Barron County, which originally was called Dallas County.

Barron became the county seat in 1868 and the first county board meeting was held the following year. Johnson House was rented for county offices. In a referendum on Nov. 4, 1873, the vote was 444-269 to move the county seat to the larger community of Rice Lake Mills.

A meeting hall was rented from Knapp, Stout & Co., one of the largest logging companies of the time in northwest Wisconsin. The company also hand-picked county officials.

But voters decided to move the county seat back to Barron in a referendum the following year. The logging company sought a court injunction to stop the move but on Dec. 29, 1874, the governor declared that Barron would be the county seat. On a cold winter night, newly elected county clerk Woodbury S. Grover hand-carried the records back to Barron. When the treasurer refused to relocate, the office was declared vacant and a new treasurer was chosen.

John Quaderer, a Barron hotel owner and former foreman with Knapp, Stout & Co., was among the leaders of the move back to Barron and the upper floor of the Quaderer Hotel was appropriated as a temporary courthouse. In April 1876, the county's first courthouse, a two-story frame building facing the creek, was completed at a cost of $2,400, which was $283 more than the county's annual tax levy. A jail was built in 1879.

But construction of county buildings didn't dampen the festering feud between Barron and Rice Lake. The county's population more than doubled during the 1880s and enough residents signed a petition in 1890 to get another referendum on moving the

**Barron County**

County seat: Barron
**Current courthouse**
  Year built: 1964
  Historic status: Not eligible due to insufficent age.

county seat.

But Barron residents scrutinized the petition and got some names thrown out because they weren't registered voters. They also persuaded 196 signers of the petition to withdraw their names. In October 1891, the Wisconsin Supreme Court ruled that the petition for a referendum didn't have enough signatures.

The same year, a contract to build a new jail in Barron was awarded to C.D. Coe. Although work was stopped for a while by an injunction brought by a Rice Lake advocate, the jail and sheriff's residence were completed in September 1892.

A new courthouse was built for $38,070 in 1901. The courthouse's entry was dressed with Portage sandstone and the superstructure was built of Menominie pressed brick. The interior was finished in red oak.

Bonds were issued for a new courthouse in 1962 and the old courthouse was demolished. The new building on the same site was completed by February 1964.

The former Barron County Courthouse, circa 1920. Photo courtesy of State Historical Society of Wisconsin (postcard collection).

Originally part of La Pointe County, Bayfield County was created in 1866 and Bayfield was named the county seat. The first courthouse was a wooden structure, which was destroyed by fire in 1883, along with most county records.

James Nader, a Madison architect who also served two terms as Madison city surveyor, was hired to build a new courthouse. The building, which used local brownstone granite, was of Neoclassical revival design and was completed in 1884.

Washburn was founded in 1892 and soon became a booming lumber town whose population quickly overtook Bayfield. Petitions were circulated among the county's property owners to change the county seat to Washburn. To get additional signatures, a plot of land was divided into 25-foot lots which were sold for $1 each.

A referendum was scheduled but the issue came to a head at a local fair in Iron River where two women were competing in a popularity contest. One contestant supported Bayfield as the county seat; the other favored Washburn. Washburn supporters wined and dined the people of Iron River, who voted for the woman supporting Washburn. In the referendum, Iron River residents also supported moving the county seat.

After the governor approved the change, a

**Bayfield County**

County seat: Washburn
**Historic courthouse**
 Year built: 1883, 1894
 Historic significance: Both 1894 and 1883 courthouses are listed in the National Register.

One of two Bayfield County historic courthouses. This one is at Washburn. The other is at Bayfield.

**Bayfield County**

**Bayfield County**

The interior of the Washburn courthouse.

caravan was sent to Bayfield to move county records to Washburn.

Bayfield supporters weren't about to concede. They sought a last minute injunction to halt the move. The injunction had to be served on the county clerk, who briefly disappeared. Washburn supporters loaded up all of the county records and furnishings, leaving the Bayfield courthouse abandoned.

A small wooden structure served as a temporary courthouse in Washburn until the current courthouse was built in 1894.

The Washburn courthouse, built in 1894-96, is a prime example of Neoclassical revival architecture. Like the courthouse built a decade earlier in Bayfield, it was constructed of local brownstone. It was topped with a domed cupola and the main entrance had a tetrastyle portico with wide steps leading up to a colonnade.

The Washburn courthouse nearly was demolished in 1969, when plans were drawn up for a new courthouse. The county board decided against it, however, when a petition against demolition was signed by 1,700 residents. Instead, the board voted to build two additions.

The Bayfield courthouse is two stories plus an attic and basement. It was constructed of local rock-faced brownstone ashlar. The main entrance is surrounded by a rectangular frame of smooth and rock-faced stone. The original staircases were removed and the interior has been remodeled.

Both Bayfield County courthouses are listed in the National Register of Historic Places.

T he first Brown County courthouse was a small log cabin adjacent to Robert Irwin's home near what is now Riverside Drive and Kress Court in Green Bay. Another courthouse was built in 1825 in Menomineeville on the Fox River and it was used until 1837, when De Pere became the county seat and the log building was moved up the frozen river from Menomineeville. A two-story frame building replaced it the following year.

**Brown County**

County seat: Green Bay
**Current courthouse**
  Year built: 1911
  Historic status: Listed in the National Register of Historic Places.

When the county seat moved to Green Bay, the county bought a two-story town hall at Adams and Doty streets, which was used until 1866, when it was sold to the St. Willebrord's congregation. A new courthouse was built at Jefferson and Cherry streets.

The dawn of the 20th Century was boom time for Brown County and the population increased by 35 percent. With a larger population, officials decided to replace the courthouse that had served the community since 1866.

A new courthouse was authorized in 1908 at a cost of $318,798. Charles E. Bell, who designed the state capitols of South Dakota and Montana, was hired as the architect and General Construction Co. of Milwaukee was hired to build it. A controversy arose over whether to install a system of clocks but the board ultimately approved the $2,726 system.

When the building was completed in 1911, an

THERE IS NO VIRTUE SO TRULY GREAT
AND GOD LIKE AS JUSTICE.

EXIT

**Brown County**

estimated 10,000 people came by horse-and-wagon to view the magnificent new structure. Besides its architecture, the courthouse also featured significant artwork.

A statue by Sidney Bedore titled "Spirit of the Northwest" was erected in 1922. It honors important figures from early Brown County history, including Nicholas Perrot and Father Claude Allouez. Perrot came to Green Bay in 1671 and gathered Indian delegates to attend a ceremony where France

"The Spirit of the Northwest"

This statue, designed by Suamico native, Sidney Bedore, and dedicated on June 10, 1931 with Governor Phillip LaFollette among the speakers, represents a Fox Indian, Claude Allouez and Nicholas Perrot.

Native Americans lived in Wisconsin for about ten thousand years before the arrival of Europeans. These original settlers were ancestors of the Winnebago, Menominee and Santee Dakota. Other tribes, such as the Fox, Sauk, Mascouten, Kickapoo, Miami and Chippewa moved into this region during the 1600's.

Father Claude Allouez, a Jesuit missionary, arrived in Green Bay in 1669. He established the St. Francis Xavier mission at what is now De Pere. The following year he led an expedition to explore the Fox and the Wisconsin rivers.

Nicholas Perrot, a French explorer and fur trader, first arrived in Green Bay about 1664. Commissioned by the Government of Canada, he took formal possession of the Bay and its surrounding land in the name of the King of France in 1689.

annexed Sault Ste. Marie and land to the west. Father Allouez, a Jesuit missionary, established a mission among the Potowatomie tribe in 1669 and later founded several other missions in the area.

The courthouse was built in Beaux Arts style with Marquette raindrop stone. It features Ionic columns, a copper-clad dome and a tower with a bell and original Seth Thomas clock.

The level of decoration becomes more sophisticated floor by floor. The first floor is simple Doric, the second floor Ionic and the third floor is done in an elaborate Corinthian style.

A mural in the rotunda painted by Franz Rohrbeck, a German-born artist from Milwaukee, depicts Jean Nicolet in 1634. Another painting of Fort Howard is based on an 1851 daguerreotype and signed "Bieberstein 1910."

The Brown County Courthouse was nominated to the National Register of Historic Places in 1976. A $10.6 million renovation project was completed in 1992. A cooling system and elevator were added and plumbing, telephone, electrical and security systems were updated. The renovation, however, did not diminish the original design.

An expansive **Brown County** courtroom, above. On the opposite page are the Bedore statue and an exterior view.

# Buffalo County

The old Buffalo County Courthouse under construction in late summer 1888. Photo from the book *Alma on the Mississippi*, Gerhard Gesell collection, State Historical Society of Wisconsin (WHi(G473)160).

Buffalo County was spawned by a clever trick of Marvin Pierce who, with his brothers, sought to dominate county politics and build a new community that would become the county seat.

In 1853, Pierce lobbied the legislature to create the new county by dividing Jackson County and to designate a non-existent community of Sand Prairie as the county seat. At the same time, Pierce's brother, James, was busy buying up land at Sand Prairie.

The first county board meeting was held in 1854 and Henry Goerke's house in Fountain City was designated as the first courthouse. Later, the courthouse would move to Fountain City's Eagle Hotel.

James Pierce was elected register of deeds and Marvin Pierce was elected the first county judge. In 1855, another brother, Wesley Pierce, was elected district attorney.

The Pierces platted a new community called Upper Fountain City, mapping out blocks, public squares and wharves. With a stray raft of timber, they erected a make-

**Buffalo County**

County seat: Alma
Current courthouse
   Year built: 1962
   Historic significance:
Not eligible due to
insufficient age.

shift courthouse for $100. By 1859, the county seat was ready for occupancy and the Pierces got a legal order that county officials must move to the designated site in their new community.

But the people of Holmes Landing had supported the county's creation with the understanding their community would be the county seat. County officials refused to move from Fountain City.

In an 1860 referendum, Fountain City won as the voters' choice for the Buffalo County seat. But Alma had received lots of votes and the Wisconsin Supreme Court decided that Alma should be the county seat.

Buffalo City won a subsequent referendum but the results were thrown out due to voting irregularities. Buffalo City is the only chartered, non-existent city in the nation. The land for the city was bought in 1855 by the Colonization Society of Cincinnati, which believed the site would be ideal for a settlement.

A courthouse was erected at Alma in 1861 and a jail was built adjacent to the courthouse in 1868. The county's second courthouse was built in 1888 and demolished in 1968. The existing courthouse was started in the summer of 1962. In 1988, the county added jail space, sheriff's offices, a garage, impound area and conference rooms.

# Burnett County

COURT HOUSE, GRANTSBURG, WIS.

**Former Burnett County Courthouse in Grantsburg, circa 1910. Photo courtesy of the State Historical Society of Wisconsin (postcard collection).**

Burnett County was named for eccentric lawyer Thomas Pendleton Burnett of Prairie du Chien. Originally part of Polk County, Burnett County was created in 1865 and Grantsburg was selected as the county seat.

Grantsburg was first settled by Canute Anderson, who spent the winter of 1852-53 along the St. Croix River north of the present city. Anderson built the area's first grist mill.

A courthouse and jail were built at the turn of the 20th Century. The extension of the Soo Line to Duluth in 1916 and later development of Highway 35 brought more settlers.

In 1976, a petition was circulated to move the county seat to a more central location and the question was on the November ballot that year. The election was later declared illegal but in 1982, another petition was circulated and voters approved moving the county seat to Meenan Township north of Siren, where the Burnett County Government Center was built.

**Burnett County**

**County seat: Siren**
**Current courthouse**
 **Year built: 1982**
 **Historic status: Not eligible due to insufficient age.**

7

Calumet County

**Calumet County**

Calumet County got its name from a Menominee Indian village on the eastern shore of Lake Winnebago. That name means peace.

Construction of the first courthouse in Chilton wasn't started until 1859, twenty-three years after Calumet County was established. The first county seat was designated by the legislature at Whitesborough, but county officials didn't know where it was so they met at Stockbridge instead. Chilton, which was founded in 1845, then became the county seat.

In 1858, the county board approved a resolution and appropriated $1,500 to build a courthouse but the decision wasn't popular with everyone. Disputes and lawsuits delayed completion of the structure until 1864. A local newspaper editorialized:

"A few politicians have been traveling the county to convince the people that they do not want a courthouse for, if it is erected, it will be likely to help Chilton; second, because it will take away a good political hobby for riding into office hereafter."

Asoph Green was hired as general contractor but he withdrew from the task when he was elected to the Assembly. George Montgomery was hired to prosecute Green for failure to complete the courthouse but ultimately the building was finished.

Calumet County's first courthouse was an el-

**Calumet County**

County seat: Chilton
**Current courthouse**
 Year built: 1913
 Historic status: Listed in the National Register of Historic Places.

egant stone building with four rooms and a safe for records and papers. Construction and furnishings cost $1,200. In 1882, the first courthouse was demolished and the stone was used in a new building.

The current Calumet County courthouse was erected in 1913 after the 1882 courthouse was destroyed by fire. It features a low center dome and concrete-trimmed brick parapet. The two upper stories are supported by the rusticated ground floor made of concrete block. A center pavilion across the front frames a shallow two-story portico with red brick pilasters. Ionic capitals and bases match the ground floor. The upper stories have sills and alternating voussoirs on the rectangular windows.

In 1976, an addition to the jail and courthouse was completed to the east and north of the original building. A second floor for the human services department was added in 1983. Another addition was completed in 1998.

The old Calumet County Jail, opposite page, was built in 1876. The building, which also had offices and living quarters for the sheriff, was demolished in 1976, when it was replaced by a courthouse and jail addition. A courthouse plaque, at right, explains the origin and meaning of the "Calumet."

Calumet County

## Chippewa County

Court House,    Chippewa Falls, Wis.

**The former Chippewa Falls County Courthouse, circa 1908. Photo courtesy State Historical Society of Wisconsin (postcard collection).**

Construction of the county's first courthouse began in 1851 but it never was finished. The first election of county officers wasn't held until 1853 and, even then, the election was arranged by a few individuals and the legislature ordered another election the following year.

In 1854, a Chippewa Falls jail was set up in H.S. Allen's root house

**Chippewa County**

County seat: Chippewa Falls
Current courthouse
   Year built: 1951
   Historic status: Not eligible due to insufficent age.

and a carpenter shop was used as a courtroom. S.N. Fuller was elected as the first county judge.

Two years later, the county board selected a courthouse site on Catholic Hill but it wasn't until 1860 that the courthouse and jail, built of pine lumber, were completed. A stone courthouse and jail replaced them in 1875. That structure was demolished in 1951, when a modern courthouse opened. An addition was built in 1991-92 to house social services offices.

Chippewa County may have been Wisconsin's most reluctant county. After the county was created by dividing Crawford County in 1845, people still traveled to Crawford County for civil and judicial matters.

In 1854, a fierce battle was under way over selection of the county seat. Contenders were O'Neill's Mills, later Neillsville, and Weston Rapids. An election was scheduled in O'Neill's Mills and voters from Weston Rapids had to cross a boom over O'Neill Creek to reach the polls.

As an election strategy, supporters of O'Neill's Mills treated partisans of Weston Rapids to whiskey so that many became too drunk to walk the boom over the creek. The result was 90 votes for O'Neill's Mills and 73 for Weston Rapids.

The vote reversed the legislature's decision of 1853, when Weston Rapids had been selected as the county seat. Samuel Weston had skillfully lobbied the Legislature to win the first round.

With the county seat question finally settled, the county board in 1856 paid $300 to James O'Neill for land and levied $2,000 for a courthouse. Edward Furlong was named general contractor with a winning bid of $1,895. The building was two stories, painted white and had a moderate-sized courtroom and one jury room. If a lawyer needed some records and the door was locked, he climbed through the window, according to R.J. MacBride, one of the first Neillsville attorneys.

A jail was built in 1866 for $1,300 of oak planks. It was replaced in 1882 and the county's third jail, which survives, was completed in 1897.

In 1876, Clark County built its second courthouse of stone. The architect was C.J. Ross of LaCrosse, who designed similar courthouses in LaCrosse and Columbia Counties. The county board appropriated $10,000 and set the maximum cost at $20,000. The heroic figure of "Justice" was placed atop the spire, although the original wooden statue later was replaced by a metal replica.

---

### Clark County

County seat: **Neillsville**
**Current courthouse**
  Year built: 1965
  Historic status: Not eligible due to insufficient age; jail listed in the National Register.

---

**The former Clark County Jail, built in 1897, now is a museum and listed in the National Register of Historic Places.**

The original courthouse was moved to Fifth Street where it was divided into apartments. A bay window was added to the old courthouse at the urging of Mrs. George Hart, who wanted to see who was coming down the street from her husband's first-floor express office.

The second courthouse was razed in 1965 and replaced.

**Clark County**

# Columbia County

## Columbia County

**County seat: Portage**
**Current courthouse**
  Year built: 1962
  Historic status: Not
eligible due to insufficient age.

Columbia County's Civil War courthouse, the second substantial courthouse in the state, was demolished in 1962, after serving the county nearly 100 years.

A new courthouse was built on the same site in 1962 and it was extensively remodeled in 1992.

In 1863, the county board levied $8,000 for a courthouse but many citizens objected because they already were paying high war taxes. The courthouse levy was boosted to $10,000, however, after a plan was presented for a $17,830 courthouse. By the time the courthouse was finished in 1865, the actual cost had escalated to $26,000.

Over the next century, steam heating replaced the original courthouse's box stoves and the building was updated with modern lighting, closets and a water system. The register of deeds moved to a

The Columbia County Courthouse, circa 1905. Photo courtesy State Historical Society of Wisconsin (postcard collection).

separate building in 1894.

The first county courthouse was built in 1851 but it burned down in 1864. A jail and sheriff's residence were completed in 1887 for $17,335.

One of the first county judges was Judge James Taylor Lewis, who settled in Columbus after he was born in New York and received his law degree in 1845. He later served as lieutenant governor and became governor in 1864.

This Crawford County Jail, built in 1843, dates back to territorial days.

# Crawford County

Prairie du Chien was an early seat of government for most of western Wisconsin. Crawford County was established as one of three territorial counties in 1818. The current courthouse was erected in 1867 after earlier structures became so unsafe that county officials abandoned them.

A building committee composed of H. Dousman, H. Beach and William Dutcher was appointed and the county purchased the entire block around the site of the old courthouse in 1866. County officials raised $10,000 from local businessmen and appropriated $15,000 in tax money for the new building.

The courthouse expresses the rectangular formality of its Italianate style but the exterior features the warm color and rough texture of locally quarried Dolomitic limestone. The original wing has two stories above a raised basement. Additions were completed in 1896 and 1931.

The territorial prison in the basement of the historic courthouse is one of the oldest and best preserved 19th Century jails in Wisconsin. The dank cells of the county's dungeon, possibly constructed in 1843, were only a few steps from the grand courtroom. Doors to the jail opened to the west and there were no emergency or secondary exits. The lower level on the north side has five 7-foot by 5-foot cells with bunk beds. Heavy iron

**Crawford County**

**County seat: Prairie du Chien**
**Current Courthouse**
  **Year built: 1867**
  **Historic status: Listed in the National Register of Historic Places.**

doors make it impossible to see out. Cells in a central corridor were used as temporary holding cells. Two cells used for solitary confinement are barely tall enough to stand in with no outside light. The cells are equipped with leg irons and chains.

The basement jail was used until 1896, when it was replaced. Now, it is used for storage.

Chairs serve instead of the usual benches in this Crawford County courtroom both for the public, above, and jurors, at right. An exterior courthouse view is on the opposite page.

**Dane County**

The Dane County Courthouse, circa 1922. The building was on the site of what now is a county-operated parking ramp. Photo courtesy of the State Historical Society of Wisconsin.

Despite an unusual cupola that crowned the roof and a portico front with classic pillars, Dane County's first courthouse was widely viewed as a lemon.

Two years after it was finished in 1851, serious leaks were reported at the base of the dome and county supervisors complained of "shoddy shingle work." A ladder that someone left on the roof was destroying some of the shingles and the basement was declared a fire hazard.

The county's first jail was a log cabin and the first inmate was a state assemblyman accused of killing a colleague.

In 1881, a report that the courthouse was burning actually turned out to be a smoldering pile of manure near the building's barn. The first courthouse was torn down three years later, when the board appropriated $134,750 for a new courthouse. The final price was $180,000 when it opened in 1886.

**Dane County**

County seat: Madison
**Current courthouse**
 Year built: 1957
 **Historic status: Not eligible due to insufficient age.**

The second courthouse was a four-story structure of red brick and sandstone. It featured red gingerbread bric-a-brac and hip-roofed peaks. A judge predicted the sturdy structure would remain in use for a century.

Actually, it was used for 71 years, until the City-County Building opened in the 1957 and an effort by some supervisors to preserve the old building failed.

By the 1920s, however, an effort had begun to build a new Dane County courthouse coinciding with city plans to replace its city hall at Mifflin Street and Wisconsin Avenue. The courthouse project resurfaced repeatedly until it died of dissension in 1936.

In 1952, $3 million in bonds were allocated for the City-County Building and construction began in March 1955. The building had 21,000 cubic yards of concrete, 200 miles of wiring and 5,000 door locks. The county jail also is housed in the building.

 A City-County Building addition of jail cells was completed in the early 1980s and the Public Safety Building, with more jail space, opened in 1994.

In the 1990s, circuit judges lobbied for a new courthouse, arguing that the City-County Building was no longer adequate for the judiciary's needs.

**Dane County**

# Dodge County

## Dodge County

**County seat: Juneau**
**Current courthouse**
  Year built: 1878, 1937, 1993
  Historic status: Old building listed in the National Register but torn down and soon to be delisted.

The original name of the Dodge County seat was Victory and later it was called Dodge Centre. In 1848, the named was changed to Juneau.

The first courthouse was a 40-foot by 60-foot structure built for $6,000. The cost included basswood shingles and two coats of paint.

In 1877, the courthouse burned to the ground and fire destroyed the county treasurer's office a year later. Those events fueled the drive for a new courthouse, which was completed in 1878 for $27,000. After accepting a bid from one architect, county officials faced charges of misuse of funds and quickly contracted with H.C. Koch and Co. of Milwaukee to design the new courthouse.

The second Dodge County courthouse featured an eclectic assemblage of Victorian motifs that complemented its tall proportions, intersecting units and mansard roof. Dominated by a central pavilion, it rose two stories plus an attic above a raised basement of rusticated brick. The mansardic tower was suggestive of Second Empire style.

The county's second courthouse survived until 1996. A stone structure was added south of the building in 1937 that doubled the building's size and the courts later were moved to a modern glass and stone building. The 1879 portion was demolished, the 1937 portion remodeled and a new structure added in 1996.

**A painting of the old Dodge County Courthouse, opposite page, by a local artist is all that remains of the historic building. The painting hangs in the county board room of the new building. Administrative offices, at left, are in an addition to the old courthouse. The design at right is repeated throughout the building.**

**Dodge County**

**Door County**

Door County Courthouse and school building. Photo courtesy State Historical Society of Wisconsin.

Increase Claflin was Door County's first white settler, establishing a homestead near Little Sturgeon in 1835. During the 1850s, mills opened on the peninsula for the logging industry.

When the county was founded, officials held the first meeting in 1856 on some fallen logs near Bailey's Harbor, where they believed the coordinates were of the location established by the legislature for the county seat.

In 1857, the county seat was changed from Gilbraltar (now Bailey's Harbor) to Graham (now Sturgeon Bay). The first county board meeting in the new county seat was held the following year.

The earliest court hearings in Door County were held in a two-story frame structure erected in 1857 as a hotel. The building, acquired by the county in 1861, housed a saloon in the basement, which was convenient when court proceedings became too dull.

In 1861, the legislature divided the county into three districts and the county board consisted of one representative from each district. According to historian Hjalmar R. Holand, the system proved corrupt.

"The system of county government by three commissioners proved very unsatisfactory and obnoxious. It permeated grave injustices in the equalization of taxes and various forms of graft," Holand wrote in *The History of Door County*.

The system was changed in 1870, just as Door County faced economic depression. When hordes of grasshoppers destroyed farm crops in 1875, county officials found it was impossible to collect taxes.

In 1878, a committee was appointed to plan a new courthouse. Plans were made by W.T. Casgrain, an engineer for the Surgeon Bay and Lake Michigan Canal Co. The estimated cost was $15,000 but the county only appropriated $12,000 so Casgrain's plan was dropped. Instead, H.C. Koch and G.A. Graebert of Milwaukee were hired to plan the courthouse.

By 1895, bad times were over as the county's magnificent scenery and location began attracting tourists, an industry that has flourished ever since.

An early Door County judge was H.M. McNally, a UW-Madison Law School graduate who had defended Joseph Allers, a transient accused of murdering 61-year-old Joseph Wuereck near Egg Harbor. Wuereck was bludgeoned to death and robbed but McNally persuaded a jury that his client was innocent.

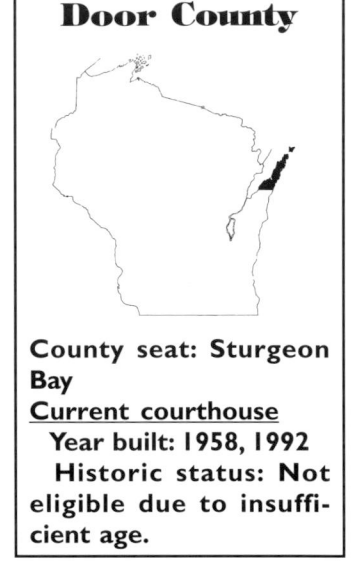

**Door County**

**County seat: Sturgeon Bay**
**Current courthouse**
 Year built: 1958, 1992
 Historic status: Not eligible due to insufficient age.

One of Douglas County's earliest settlers was Henry M. Rice, who came in 1847 to prospect for copper. Rice's Point is named after him. The county itself was named after U.S. Senator Stephen Douglas of Illinois. The senator was an investor in Douglas County land and got a large sum for his interest, which he sold before the panic of 1857.

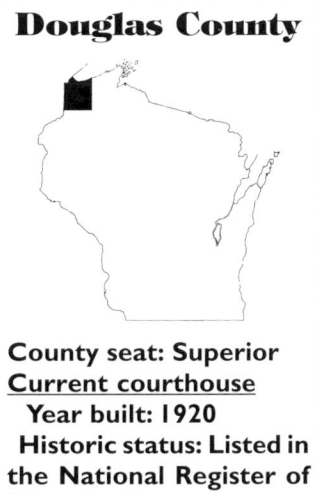

**Douglas County**

**County seat: Superior**
**Current courthouse**
   Year built: 1920
   Historic status: Listed in the National Register of Historic Places.

Before 1871, court in Douglas County was held in a three-story frame building on Superior's West Second Street.

When Douglas County was carved out of LaPointe County in 1854, the legislation that created the county specified the precise site of the county seat. Throughout the final decades of the 19th Century, Superior and West Superior warred over which would be the county seat. Superior had been designated the county seat when the county was established. In 1889, legislation to move the county seat lost on a tie vote. Residents in 1896 gathered a 100-page petition in another unsuccessful effort to relocate the county seat.

The first courthouse was built in 1871 on Newton Avenue between Fifth and Sixth streets. A jail was built in 1887 and small wings were added to the courthouse in 1896 and 1897.

By 1920, the Douglas County population had grown to 75,000 and the county opened a new court-

Douglas County

**Douglas County**

house that was built for $596,564. Four years earlier, the legislature had finally passed a bill allowing the county board to hold a referendum on where to place the county seat.

The new building, hailed at the time as the finest courthouse in the Northwest, was listed in the National Register of Historic Places in 1987.

It is made of Bedford blue cut stone. A monumental Neoclassical structure, the Douglas County courthouse has a colossal Ionic colonnade on the exterior. The vestibule is wainscoted with Pavanazza marble from Italian quarries. The 100-foot by 40-foot main rotunda has columns of solid concrete encased in marble. Entrance doors are of heavy copper and lighting is provided by 600-pound chandeliers. Bronze clocks in the corridors can be seen from any position on any floor.

County records were destroyed when the first Dunn County courthouse burned at Dunnville in 1858. The county seat was moved three years later to Menomonie and court was held in the "Charley Waller Building," which had a courtroom upstairs. The court moved to a building later used as a newspaper office after the Waller Building offices

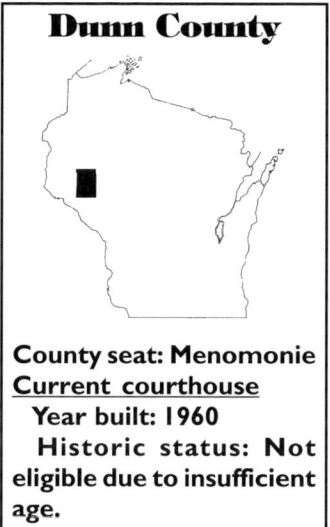

**Dunn County**

County seat: Menomonie
**Current courthouse**
  Year built: 1960
  Historic status: Not eligible due to insufficient age.

were burglarized and $100 was stolen.

In 1872, Canute Thompson built a basic courthouse for $6,000 but the inside fittings boosted the cost to $45,000. It was a substantial brick building in the center of a square that occupied an entire block on land donated by William Wilson. The architect was A.J. Kinney.

Bricks for the courthouse were made on the grounds and in Wilson Park, using clay hauled from beds on the outskirts of the city.

The county's first jail also burned down and, when the county seat moved, a second jail built in 1858 was moved to Menomonie in pieces and reconstructed.

The county's latest courthouse, a Y-shaped building with three wings, was finished in 1960 and

**The 1872 Dunn County Courthouse. Photo courtesy of Wilfred Harris.**

cost $903,624.

The county's first murder of a white man occurred in 1844. A suspect was arrested but acquitted after a trial in Prairie du Chien.

**Dunn County**

**Eau Claire County**

Before the second Eau Claire County Courthouse was built in 1873, Judge W.P. Bartlett sent a delegation of planners around the state to borrow the best ideas of other county designs. The brick structure, covered with stone trim, cost $75,000. The building replaced a wooden structure at Wilson Park that had been used since 1862. The wooden courthouse was moved and became a boarding house.

For 102 years until it was razed in 1975, the second courthouse served as the focal point for the community. When labor disputes erupted in 1881 between lumber company owners and mill hands, the courthouse front lawn became the headquarters of the state militia. About 150 victims of a major 1884 flood came to the courthouse for aid.

After a system of fire alarm boxes failed, a 2,500-pound bell was installed in the courthouse tower to sound the warning. The bell wasn't loud enough so it was shipped back to Milwaukee in 1887 in exchange for a larger one.

In 1935, farmers were given a drought relief project of remodeling the courthouse entrance. The courthouse annex was replaced in 1953 and a new courthouse completed in 1973. In 1993, a $3.6 million courthouse addition was approved.

Two Eau Claire lawyers decided in 1857 that they weren't getting enough business and decided to create their own case. They accused a farmer of stealing a pig he had brought to town to sell. One lawyer served as prosecutor, the other as defense attorney.

Pitt Bartlett, the defense attorney, advised his client to stand near the door with his hat in his hand so, if the jury found him guilty, he could take off. When the jury delivered its guilty verdict, the farmer fled immediately down Barstow Street to Main, then to a steamboat landing where he waded across the river. He was pursued by the lawyers, jury and witnesses but they lost him in the woods.

Eau Claire's first murder occurred a year later, when Andrew Seitz, who boarded with Charles Naither, squabbled with his landlord over doing the dishes and a $5.50 debt. Naither was thrown downstairs, but returned with a knife and killed Sietz.

**Eau Claire County**

County seat: Eau Claire
Current courthouse
    Year built: 1973
    Historic status: Not eligible due to insufficient age.

The former Eau Claire County Courthouse, circa 1910. Photo courtesy of State Historical Society of Wisconsin (postcard collection).

Iron ore discovered in 1873 led to the settlement of Florence County. The county and city were named after the Florence Mine, which took its name from the wife of Dr. H.P. Hulst, an early mining expert from Iron Mountain, Michigan.

After Florence County was created in 1882, land was bought for a courthouse for $925 from the Pewaubie Land Co. More than a half dozen courthouse designs were offered before the one by James E. Clancy of Antigo was selected.

The solid brick courthouse was built in a Romanesque Revival style with Wisconsin sandstone and blue limestone trimmings. Its wide steps lead to a north entrance and the 40-foot walls are topped by a high-pitched roof with round turrets. In the northwest corner, a tower rises to 65 feet. The cost was $13,000 plus $4,000 for a matching jail with three cells. The contractors were Wickert & Weber.

A copy of *The Mining News,* a silver coin and lists of county officials, firefighters and others were placed under the cornerstone.

On Feb. 6, 1908, fire caused about $3,000 damage to the treasurer's office and a quick response by volunteer firefighters prevented the entire courthouse from burning down. The ground floor offices were remodeled and a bigger vault was installed. The interior was remodeled in 1915. A vestibule was added to the north entrance in 1921.

Few structural changes were made between 1922 and 1941, when the courthouse tower was dismantled and replaced with a flat roof. A grant was received in 1963 to build an addition along with a highway department shed.

### Florence County

County seat: Florence
**Current courthouse**
  Year built: 1897
  Historic status: Listed in the National Register of Historic Places.

Despite the roof remodeling, the Florence County courthouse was added to the National Register of Historic Places in December 1984. A 10,000-square-foot addition was built in 1994.

The Florence County Courthouse, of a simpler design than elaborate structures in some other counties, is listed in the National Register of Historic Places. Photo courtesy of State Historical Society of Wisconsin, Historic Preservation Unit.

Florence County

**Fond du Lac County**

Contractor Issac Brown finished the first three-story Fond du Lac County courthouse in 1850. The first floor was stone and the upper stories were wood. On the lower floor of the 40-foot by 90-foot building, the northern half was the jail and the southern half was the jailer's residence. The second floor housed county offices and a courtroom was on the third floor. The building had a modest steeple and a flag staff.

A small stone building was erected for records of the register of deeds and clerk of courts.

In 1868, citizens began to agitate for a new courthouse. A new jail was built instead but the original courthouse burned down in 1881. For three years, the courts operated in temporary quarters until a new courthouse was completed in 1884.

J.H. Green was the architect for the second $62,000 courthouse, which featured a clock tower. The red-brick building with Victorian accents and several spires was erected on the same site as the first courthouse. The third-floor courtroom served as a gathering place for conventions, caucuses, church services and lectures.

A $92,000 addition was completed in 1926. In 1965, the clock tower was removed as an alternative to repairing it. By this time, the decorative chimneys and 18 fireplaces also were long gone and the roof leaked.

The county's second courthouse was demolished in November 1981 and replaced by the $10 million Fond du Lac City-County Government Center.

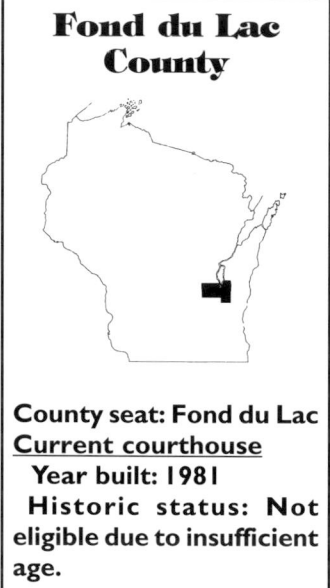

**Fond du Lac County**

County seat: Fond du Lac
**Current courthouse**
 Year built: 1981
 Historic status: Not eligible due to insufficient age.

G 30426 Court House, Fond Du Lac, Wis.

**The Fond du Lac County Courthouse, circa 1905-1910. Photo courtesy of the State Historical Society of Wisconsin (postcard collection).**

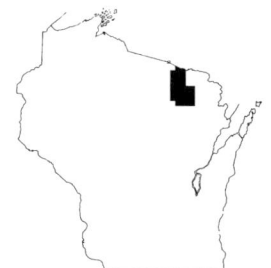

**Forest County**

County seat: Crandon
**Current courthouse**
 Year built: 1912
 Historic status: Not eligible due to loss of integrity.

Forest County's courthouse and jail, completed in 1912. Photo courtesy of the State Historical Society of Wisconsin, negative WHi(W6)23683.

Attorney and businessman Samuel Shaw founded Crandon in 1885, naming the community after Frank P. Crandon, the tax commissioner of the Chicago & North Western Railroad. Although Crandon was designated the county seat, North Crandon (now Argonne) became the population center.

The settlement rush to Forest County didn't come until the dawn of the twentieth century. In the 1890s, Crandon's population was 250. A decade later, the population had swollen to 2,000.

Forest County was created from parts of Oconto and Langlade counties. But it wasn't until 1901 that the railroad's arrival brought a large influx of immigrants from the hills of Kentucky hoping to find work in the lumber mills. It was then that Forest County, with high ridges and moraines left by the glacier, became known as Little Kentucky.

Some of the immigrants were fugitives from the law.

Crandon was incorporated in 1908. Before 1909, a two-story frame building served as Forest County's justice center. A new courthouse, featuring a clock tower, along with the jail and sheriff's residence, were completed in 1912 at a cost of $55,000.

*Forest County*

# Grant County

The Grant County Courthouse, above, is one of Wisconsin's most highly prized historic treasures. On the opposite page are views of a courtroom entrance and through the glass dome.

**Grant County**

County seat: Lancaster
Current courthouse
Year built: 1902
Historic status: Listed in the National Register of Historic Places.

The current Grant County courthouse, one of Wisconsin's most prized historic treasures, was begun in 1902. The architect was Henry C. Koch, an important pioneer architect from Milwaukee.

Koch said the dome was inspired by St. Peter's Cathedral in Rome. The octagonal glass dome is rare but not unique and may have been a stock item. The dome is identical to one in Oneida County. The building, with its fluted brownstone pilasters, is an example of relatively abstract Neoclassicism and a nine-element Civil War monument is located on the northeast corner of the square.

The three-story courthouse, built in 1902, has brick walls, Lake Superior brownstone trim, belt courses and window pediments. Three types of brick were used in the exterior walls, including red clay brick for the basement, glazed brown bricks for the first floor and light-brown bricks for the upper stories.

Light filters through the glass dome to illuminate the three-story interior. Unlike other courthouses, the glass dome survived Wisconsin's variable weather. Four Doric columns support the second floor and four Ionic columns support the third floor.

On the grounds are eight small Civil War monuments surrounding a large vertical monument.

These are Wisconsin's first Civil War monuments, dedicated on July 4, 1867. At the northwest corner of the square is a fountain with a statue of a Civil War soldier holding his rifle.

The first Grant County courthouse, 36-feet-square, was completed in 1838, but the county also needed a jail. A $400 contract was let to Harvey Pepper to build a log jail. A stone jail replaced the log building in 1844 but the $1,685 building was

# Grant County

A statue of Nelson Dewey, above, outside the courthouse and artifacts inside the G.A.R. museum, at right. On the opposite page are views of the museum entrance and of the glass dome exterior.

badly ventilated.

By 1851, the courthouse had become dilapidated and in 1853 a small stone building was erected to protect the county's records from fire.

In 1872, a $20,500 contract was awarded to Hough & Co. of Indianapolis to build a 12-cell jail with a gallery.

In 1881, Nick Ames, a 15-year-old, was a suspect in several burglaries. When police went to arrest him, Ames asked that he be allowed to take his horses and wagon home first but he took off instead. The burglaries of grocery stores and a milliner shop continued. When the brazen burglar stole a gold coin from the treasurer's office, the sheriff followed candle drippings up the stairs to the courthouse attic, where Ames was discovered sleeping under a quilt in the corner.

Ames persuaded deputies to lock him in a corridor instead of a cell and escaped again. The burglaries continued as Ames was recaptured but escaped once again. Finally, he was sentenced to prison but the burglaries started right

up again when he was paroled. He was captured in 1891 in a cave near Dutch Hollow, but the law still couldn't hold him. He finally got another prison term.

Green County

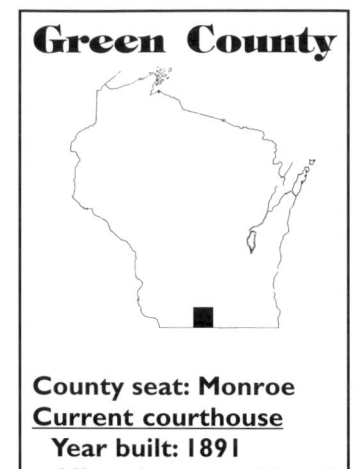

The first Green County courthouse was a 20-by-30 frame building. Before it was completed in 1840, it burned to the ground. A year later, Demas Beach was given $400 to put up a building on the southwest corner of the square with the second floor reserved for government offices. The building later became the American House ho-

**County seat: Monroe**
**Current courthouse**
  **Year built: 1891**
  **Historic status: Listed in the National Register of Historic Places.**

tel.

William Dunten of Rochester in Racine County was hired in 1844 to build another Green County courthouse for $3,500. The colonial-style building featured four two-story pillars and a bell from a local church. A fence was erected to keep out wandering livestock.

Although it was picturesque, the courthouse eventually became too small and it was sold in 1891 for $100.

Before a new courthouse was built, Monticello offered 10 acres and a $65,000 fund-raising campaign if that community could become the county seat. A Monticello teacher apparently organized the campaign, which ultimately fizzled.

The county board approved a new courthouse by a 11-10 vote. C.S. Mansfield of Freeport, a disciple of the concepts of Henry

**A flag waves in front of the Green County Courthouse, above. A mural adds to courtroom decor, opposite page, and clock doctor Nick Speck is at work.**

**Green County**

Hobson Richardson, was hired as architect.

The two-and-a-half story courthouse has a high basement, hipped roof and four corner towers. The southwest tower roof was removed in 1955 and replaced with a flat roof. The main tower is partially free-standing with four clock faces framed in rock-faced limestone voussoirs.

Masonry walls are made of red brick from Maiden Rock. The base and exterior are trimmed in white limestone rock-faced ashlar. Smooth-faced limestone was used to trim some horizontal belt courses. The east and west facades feature shallow limestone porches with marble colonnades over the building's two main entrances.

The interior has lower level offices, main level offices and a second-floor courtroom and associated offices. The main-level, 100-foot corridor has a checkered tile floor and oak wainscoting. The large courtroom spans the length of the entire floor from north to south.

Monroe and Green County split the cost of a tower clock in 1892. Ice and snow occasionally freezes on the three-foot exposed minute hand, which clock doctor Nick Speck characterized as "frostbite of the hand."

The tower turret was removed and capped with concrete in 1955 after high winds ripped sheet metal off the steeple.

**From hanging lights to the checkered tile floor, the Green County Courthouse projects a stately image.**

# Green Lake County

J ames Powell, who settled at Green Lake in 1835, is one of Green Lake County's earliest settlers. Nathan Strong founded the village of Strongville, which later became Berlin. Green Lake, then called Dartford, and Berlin battled over which should be the county seat. Another early settler was a Mr. Pomeroy, who was described as a relative of novelist James Fennimore Cooper. Pomeroy later moved to Cooperstown, N.Y.

**Green Lake County**

County seat: Green Lake
**Current courthouse**
   Year built: 1899
   Historic status: Listed in the National Register of Historic Places.

The first courthouse was built at Dartford, but as the courthouse facilities deteriorated during the 1890s, Berlin residents launched a campaign to relocate the county seat. In 1898, citizens voted to keep the county seat at Dartford and construction of the county's current courthouse began the following year.

By the time of the county seat battle, a second generation of settlers was in control of local government. Many people attended old settlers' meetings, where they reminisced about the difficulties of frontier life before the then-modern era.

At one of these meetings in 1882, more than 3,000 people attended and Judge D. J. Pulling was the featured speaker. He talked about how difficult it was for early settlers to relocate in what then was a wilderness.

"Those who know only of the present time, of the railroad and the telegraph, can never appreciate the nerve, the courage, the heroism required for such an undertaking," he said.

One of the first lawsuits involved an assault and battery case. After presentation of the evidence, the jury retired under the supervision of a local constable, who had been a witness in the case. In an effort to arrive at a verdict, the jury asked the constable to testify again. When they still couldn't reach a decision, jurors decided to use a game of "high, low, jack" to render the guilty verdict.

**A view of the community outside from between the columns.**

The Iowa County courthouse, designed by Ernest Wiesen of Mineral Point, is the oldest in continuous use in the state. The two-story structure was built in 1859 in temple Greek Revival style with buff Galena limestone from local quarries. The stone work was done by Cornish workmen with blocks so closely fitted that little mortar was needed.

**Iowa County**

**County seat: Dodgeville**
**Current courthouse**
  **Year built: 1859**
  **Historic status: Listed in the National Register of Historic Places.**

A white, two-story portico with a massive pediment is beneath an octagonal cupola. Doric columns, inclined inward, were inspired by the Parthenon. The front entrance of carved stone is supported by pilasters and a similar pediment is found at the side entrance. Mutins were removed from the windows before 1959 so each now has a single pane. The original bell cracked while ringing at midnight on the Fourth of July in 1898.

Several alterations include an 1894 addition that used matching stone and a second addition in 1927. Due to deterioration, the portico was restored in 1937 with duplication of mouldings and millwork from samples of the originals. The interior also has been altered since the original portion was built.

Iowa County was established before statehood. Among the first official acts of the territorial county court were the granting of divorces in 1837 to John and Mary McArthur and to A.W. and Eleanor Floyd.

Beatings often sufficed as the quickest form of frontier justice.

The first courthouse was a twenty-foot-square, two-story log structure built for $575 in 1835 at Mineral Point, then the county seat. A second courthouse was built at Mineral Point for $7,468 in 1842. When the county seat was moved to Dodgeville in 1858 after two referendums and a political battle, a new courthouse was needed.

The most sensational early case was the murder of Samuel Southwick by William Caffee in 1842. Caffee was among the guests

**Iowa County**

at a housewarming party hosted by Southwick, who apparently liked to organize his social affairs down to the finest detail. Southwick had prepared a list of dancers and, as he called off their names, Caffee became offended. He grabbed the list out of Southwick's hand and fled outside with the host in pursuit. Southwick was armed with a stick and threatened to knock down Caffee if he didn't return the list. Caffee pulled out a

pistol and killed Southwick.

Caffee, who threatened to escape, was shackled with leg irons fashioned by the local blacksmith and watched by four armed guards. A large crowd turned out to watch his execution and, as he approached the gallows, an unrepentent Caffee said he would like a raw slice of the judge's heart to eat.

Moses M. Strong, Caffee's defense attorney, had a reputation as one of the most eloquent speakers of his day. He was a delegate to the constitutional convention and served as Assembly speaker. Leuman M. Strong, no relation to Moses Strong, served ten years as county judge and also in the legislature.

**Green County attorney Thomas J. Kelley, above, enters the Iowa County Courthouse beneath the towering columns. A judge's bench is at left.**

The Iron County courthouse was built as a town hall for the Town of Vaughn, which then was part of Ashland County. In an era when most town halls were simple one-story or two-story buildings, the Vaughn town hall was to be a $27,303 structure. The architect was L.H. Ruggles and the builders were Julius Rinke and E.J. Carroll.

**Iron County**

**County seat: Hurley**
**Historic courthouse**
  **Year built: 1892**
  **Historic status: Listed in the National Register of Historic Places.**

When construction began in 1892, efforts to form the county from parts of Ashland and Oneida counties were pending in the legislature and a newspaper story in the *Montreal City Miner* indicated the building could have a multi-purpose future. The story said it would house "apartments for the fire department, a city jail, rooms for the town offices, a large room that might be used for a court room or for any public gathering — in fact, the building would serve for county purposes, and many counties in the state have nowhere near as fine a building as this will be."

Iron County was created in March 1893 and the courthouse was finished five months later. The town relinquished most space in the building for county offices, reserving the right to use the court

**A corner tower dominates the Iron County Courthouse.**

**Iron County**

room for public meetings if those meetings didn't conflict with county functions.

The building now is owned by the Iron County Historical Society.

A drill core 5½ feet in diameter is displayed near the courthouse as a visible reminder of the importance of mining to Iron County. The drill core came from the Cary mine shaft 2,400 feet below the surface. The shaft was drilled from 1942 to 1944 and later enlarged to 13-feet by 21-feet. Men, supplies and iron ore were transported through the shaft.

**A flag reflects in a courthouse window, at left. The drill core is displayed above.**

The first Jackson County courthouse was built in 1857, four years after the county was created, on Van Buren Street in Black River Falls. But a fire destroyed the building before it was finished. A second courthouse was built in 1862 but the building apparently appeared cheap to many citizens and it eventually was sold and moved to another location.

**Jackson County**

**County seat: Black River Falls**

**Current Courthouse**
 Year built: 1878, 1937
 Historic status: Not currently eligible due to loss of integrity.

The county's current courthouse was built in 1878 along with a jail. In 1906, a bronze fountain was created on the courthouse lawn that depicted a crane with its head erect and water coming from its beak.

The courthouse tower was removed in 1937 and an addition was erected to the north. In 1960, a new jail replaced the 1878 structure and, in 1986, the law enforcement center replaced the 1960 jail. A new courtroom, jury room, judge's office and conference rooms were part of the 1986 addition.

The Jackson County Courthouse, circa 1890. Photo by C.J. Van Schaick. Photo courtesy of State Historical Society of Wisconsin, neg. WHi (V2) 29.

**Jackson County**

# Jefferson County

When Wisconsin was a territory, court was held in Jefferson House and on the second floor of the Sanborn Building. In 1842, fire damaged the Sanborn Building and William Sanborn got a contract to build a courthouse. He contracted with George Crist and Daniel N. Miller to construct the courthouse, jail and sheriff's residence on a public square.

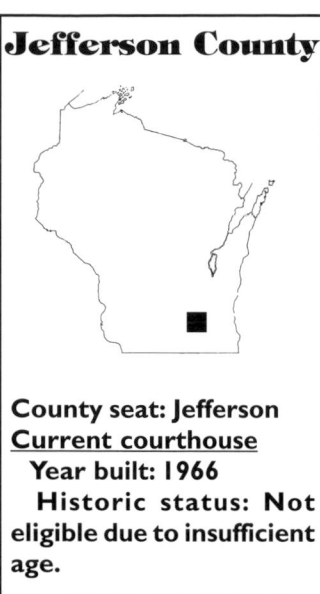

**Jefferson County**

**County seat: Jefferson**
**Current courthouse**
  **Year built: 1966**
  **Historic status: Not eligible due to insufficient age.**

The 30-foot by 40-foot courthouse, completed in 1843 at a cost of $3,000, included county offices and jury rooms on the first floor and a courtroom on the second floor. A log jail was built the same year.

In 1850, a brick jail was built and it burned down twenty-four years later. In 1861, a courthouse addition was erected. A massive brick, two-and-a-half story jail was completed for $18,000 in 1875. The current courthouse was constructed in 1966 and a jail addition was built in 1991.

Jefferson County's most famous murder case in recent years was the conviction of Diane Borchardt for the contract murder of her husband, Ruben. Ironically, another man named Borchardt was killed in one of the county's first murders.

In 1874, Borchardt's stepdaughter, Johannah, went to Charles Borchardt's home and said a stranger had hit Charles' father on the head. A post-

JEFFERSON COUNTY COURT HOUSE, JEFFERSON, WIS.

The Jefferson County Courthouse, circa 1910. Photo courtesy of State Historical Society of Wisconsin (postcard collection).

mortem determined that the elder Borchardt in fact had died of three blows to the head and a bloody hammer found on the premises turned suspicion on the family.

The elder Borchardt's wife and her daughter, Wilhelmina, were taken into custody. Justice C. M. Ducasse bound the wife over from trial but released the daughter. But the girl was arrested again after more evidence was found.

At the trial, one damning piece of evidence was a threatening letter that Wilhelmina had written to Johannah from jail: "You have always sworn against me and my mother and, if you persist in doing so, mother will tell the whole story."

Even though the elder Borchardt was described as drunken and quarrelsome, Wilhelmina and her mother were sentenced to life in prison.

**A courtroom mural symbolizes pioneer days.**

Like many other Wisconsin counties, Juneau County had its own battle over the county seat, which raged for two decades after the first meeting of the county board at New Lisbon in November 1857. Voters approved New Lisbon as the county seat over Mauston in 1859 by a vote of 1,520-1,022. But the Wisconsin Supreme Court overturned the referendum results several years later, citing election irregularies, and Mauston was designated as the county seat. A resolution to build a courthouse in Mauston was approved in 1874.

The first courthouse, completed the following year, was a two-story stone structure with a tower. The building was razed in 1938, when the county board approved a plan to construct on the same site "one of the most beautiful and modern public buildings in Wisconsin."

The second Juneau County courthouse was fewer than 50 years old when it was listed in the National Register of Historic Places in 1982. Its significance lies in the fact that it is the most important Works Progress Administration structure built during the Great Depression in Juneau County. Other area WPA projects were limited to road and dam improvements.

A reinforced concrete structure of modernistic design, the courthouse has stylized geometric

**Juneau County**

**County seat: Mauston**
**Current courthouse:**
 **Year built: 1938**
 **Historic status: Listed in**
**the National Register of**
**Historic Places.**

*Juneau County*

ornament and a richly colored and textured quartzite veneer. Original windows have been replaced by smaller panes surrounded by stucco-like composition panels. However, the original window openings have been preserved.

Peter Baupre, a fur trader, was the area's first white settler, coming to what is now Mauston in 1810. When W. McAllister, Hiram Elmore and James B. McNeil built a dam and sawmill in 1842, the land north of the Lemonweir River was still controlled by the Menominees. The current site of New Lisbon was a winter stopping place while Indian men went north for hunting and trapping. The ancient Indian name for New Lisbon was Wa Du Shuda, which means "leave your canoe here."

Juneau County was created from western Adams County in 1857, the same year that the railroad was completed from Portage City to New Lisbon. The coming of the railroad brought rapid growth to New Lisbon, which soon had a population of 2,500 and eight hotels.

**Flowers and shrubs soften the hard lines of the Depression-era Juneau County Courthouse.**

**Kenosha County**

**Kenosha County**

County seat: Kenosha
**Current courthouse**
Year built: 1925
Historic status: Listed in
the National Register of
Historic Places.

The historic Kenosha County Courthouse is known for its striking murals.

A mural by A.E. Foringer symbolizes the Civil War with the inscription, "Uphold the Fight." Other murals symbolize "Knowledge" and "Power." Other figures include "Mercury" and "Force" with the quotation "Prevent the Wrong" on a tablet.

With the creation of Kenosha County in 1850, a red brick courthouse was built for $10,500. The

**An abundance of columns gives the Kenosha County Courthouse a classic appearance.**

one-and-a-half story building had a courtroom on the main floor with a gallery around it.

The building was razed in 1885 when a second courthouse and jail were completed for $31,000. In 1918, county officials began talking about a third courthouse, which was completed in 1925.

Architects Lindl, Kiser and Schutte designed the 1925 courthouse of gray Indiana limestone. The three-story structure included county offices on the first floor, courtrooms on the second floor and the county board room and teachers' quarters on the third floor.

The most famous early case in Kenosha County was the execution of John McCaffrey, which led to passage of Wisconsin's ban on capital punishment. McCaffrey was an Irish immigrant who came to America during the 1840s potato famine. By 1850, he was 30 years old and married to Bridget. The couple fought constantly.

On July 22, 1850, neighbors heard loud, angry shouts in the middle of the night and, the next day, Bridget's body was found at the bottom of a cistern. McCaffrey was found guilty of first degree murder and hanged on May 21, 1851.

On the scaffold, McCaffrey apologized for the murder but the worst part came afterward when the condemned man took a long time to die. Newspaper editor Latham Sholes was so horrified by the scene that he ran for the legislature and campaigned for a ban on capital punishment, which was enacted a few years afterward.

**Wall portraits and wood, above, decorate a Kenosha County courtroom while an expansive square rotunda, at right, is a central feature.**

An 1836 gold rush brought people flocking to Kewaunee County and skyrocketed the cost of land to $1,000 an acre but the gold rush literally didn't pan out.

The first courthouse was built in 1873 for $12,000. A $35,000 addition was finished in 1902 and the courthouse was enlarged in 1938 for $68,000.

The historic jail, built in 1876, now is a museum operated by the Kewaunee County Historical Society and is listed in the National Register of Historic Places.

West Kewaunee originally was known as Coryville and was named after Albert Cory, the first county judge and one of the earliest settlers.

Another early settler was Louis Bruemmer, who came to Wisconsin in April 1854 and worked in a sawmill at Two Rivers. After serving in the Civil War, he returned to Mishicot, where he worked as a teacher and served as town clerk and justice of the peace. He moved to Ahnapee, where he ran a succession of businesses, including a brewery, hotel, gristmill and sawmill.

Bruemmer served as county board chairman and then a decade as town clerk. A few years be-

**Kewaunee County**

**County seat: Kewaunee**
**Current courthouse**
   **Year built: 1873, 1902, 1938**
   **Historic status: Not eligible due to loss of integrity; jail is listed on the National Register.**

Court House, Kewaunee, Wis.

**The Kewaunee County Courthouse, circa 1908. Photo courtesy of State Historical Society of Wisconsin (postcard collection).**

fore his death in 1904, he was elected county judge and also worked as a bank cashier.

Despite his important contributions to Kewaunee County, Bruemmer's last days were unhappy ones. He was committed to Dewey Sanitarium in Wauwatosa after he was reported suffering from "melancholia." After promising that he wouldn't commit suicide, Bruemmer wandered away from the sanitarium and hung himself from a tree in a nearby wooded ravine.

Bruemmer had nine children and his son, Otto, became a prominent Kewaunee County attorney, serving a decade as county board chairman, Kewaunee mayor, city attorney and school board member.

*Kewaunee County*

In 1851, a two-story frame building was erected to serve as La Crosse County's first courthouse. The 26-foot by 36-foot building had county offices on the first floor and a courtroom on the second floor.

Court House, La Crosse, Wis.

**The La Crosse County Courthouse, circa 1910. Photo courtesy of State Historical Society of Wisconsin.**

By 1867, county officials realized the courthouse was too small and it was sold to a man who moved it and converted it into a boarding house. Later, it was turned into the Washington Hotel.

A one-story log jail, built flush against the courthouse, failed to keep inmates confined. It was built on sand and prisoners had an easy time digging out beneath the walls to freedom.

A new jail, modeled after ancient Egyptian architecture, was built in 1858. The 45-foot by 67-foot building had a curved cornice and 16 cells.

In 1868, the county's second courthouse was completed by contractor William Listman. It featured 16-foot exterior walls and fireproof vaults. The 60-foot-square limestone building, which cost $36,000 plus $4,000 for furnishings, had nine rooms on the first floor for county offices and a second-floor courtroom with rising seats and good acoustics. Joliet stone was used for caps and cornices and a tall spire with a statue of the blind goddess of justice on top crowned the building.

A third courthouse was built in 1904 and the 1868 courthouse was torn down. The fourth courthouse was constructed in 1964 and the 1904 courthouse was razed the following year. The county's fifth courthouse opened in 1997 and the 1964 courthouse was converted to an administration building.

One of La Crosse County's earliest murders occurred in 1852, when William Watts killed David Darst over $80 that Darst claimed Watts owed him. Darst assaulted Watts over the money but Watts grabbed an ax, striking a fatal blow under Darst's ear. Then Watts robbed Darst and dumped his body on a bluff, where it was soon discovered by a neighbor who had an appointment with the dead man.

**La Crosse County**

**County seat: La Crosse**
**Current courthouse**
 **Year built: 1997**
 **Historic status: Not eligible due to insufficient age.**

Lead mines brought the first settlers to Lafayette County and provided its earliest industry. Today, agriculture has replaced mining and the county has more than a thousand farms, averaging nearly 300 acres each.

Lafayette was split from Iowa County in 1847 and the first courthouse was built in 1853 at Shullsburg on donated land. Establishing the county seat at Shullsburg, however, angered residents in the central part of the county and, in 1857, the county board petitioned the legislature to annex the village of Avon to Darlington and establish the county seat there. After several years of debate, the legislature approved the move in 1861. Shullsburg residents appealed to the courts and the issue wasn't settled until 1866.

The Shullsburg courthouse was used as a private school and two wings later were added. It became a public school in 1868 and was burned to the ground in 1900 by a fire that originated in the chemistry department.

Even before the county seat question was settled, Lafayette County's second courthouse was erected in Darlington in 1861. The structure served the county until the current courthouse was completed in 1905.

The Lafayette County courthouse, with its magnificent dome, was a gift from Matthew Murphy,

**Lafayette County**

County seat: Darlington
**Current courthouse**
  Year built: 1905
  Historic status: Listed in the National Register. of Historic Places

*Lafayette County*

who left 70 percent of his estate to build the $136,000 structure when he died in 1903. A bust of Matthew Murphy is over the front entrance.

Murphy's parents, Dennis and Elizabeth, settled in Benton in 1827 and opened one of the area's first sawmills. Elizabeth died in 1842, leaving Dennis with four children.

Matthew Murphy was a pioneer lawyer who also worked as a surveyor. He held most local offices at one time or another, including county board chairman. He helped established Masonic lodges in southwestern Wisconsin and became one of the first officers and stockholders of the State Bank of Benton.

Some of the money Murphy provided came from a Civil War trust fund established to benefit

widows and children but never used. The fund wasn't needed after the federal government took responsibility for war victims and the money was put in Murphy's charge. He invested it and, shortly before his death, became determined that it be used to build a courthouse.

The Lafayette County courthouse, with its towering cupola and indigenous buff limestone construction, is an example of abstract Neoclassical style that characterized many Mid-

**Matthew Murphy, at left, father of the Lafayette County Courthouse, above. A view through the dome is on the opposite page.**

western courthouses designed during the first two decades of the twentieth century. The structure is three stories with a hipped roof and Ionic colonettes framing four windows on the cupola. Clock faces are on top of each window. One of Wisconsin's last lynchings took place on the courthouse lawn.

# Lafayette County

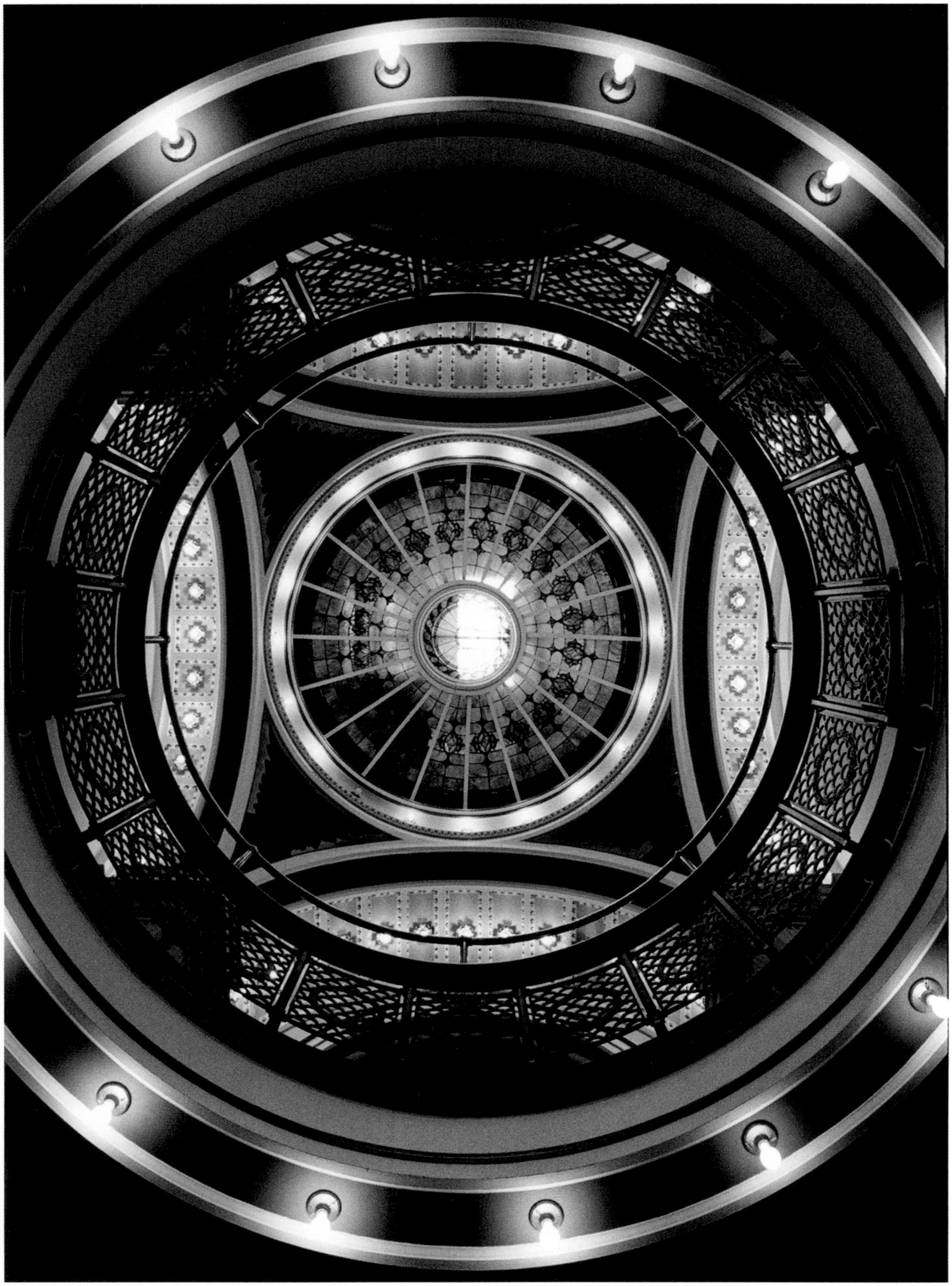

# Langlade County

**W**ithout a great deal of imagination, the state legislature established Langlade County in 1879 as the "County of New." The name was changed a year later and the first courthouse, a frame building, was completed in 1882.

The original frame courthouse was replaced by the current structure in 1905. The architects were Frank W. Kinney and Menno S. Detweiler of Minneapolis.

Murals feature the work of Axel Edward Soderberg, a Swedish artist and graduate of the Academy at Copenhagen, Denmark. Soderberg, who decorated the Swedish king's summer palace in Uppsala, came to the United States to decorate one of the buildings for the Columbian Exposition in Chicago. He was hired by Odin Oyen and settled in La Crosse, where he gained a reputation as a figure painter. His wife, Katherine Ryerson, modeled for many of his female figures.

Although the courthouse is similar to the Lafayette County courthouse in Darlington, it is less elaborate because the architects were forced by a building committee to change their designs in order to cut costs.

**Langlade County**

County seat: Antigo
**Current courthouse**
  Year built: 1905
  Historic status: Listed in the National Register of Historic Places.

*Langlade County*

A Vietnam war memorial, opposite page, is on the courthouse grounds while ornate doorknob detail is shown at left. The mural above on the courtroom wall depicts the biblical story of Daniel and the oak and sycamore tree. A complete view of the courtroom is at right.

## Lincoln County

**M**errill was founded in 1847 when Andrew Warren began building a dam across the Wisconsin River.

County officials decided to build a courthouse in 1876, two years after Lincoln County was separated from Marathon County, but it took until 1880 to finish it. During the intervening years, court was held in a building on Merrill's Main Street owned by T. B. Gallagher.

A site was purchased for $1,200 and the courthouse was built that later became the Lincoln County Training School.

A new courthouse was begun in 1903 but labor trouble slowed construction of the 98-foot by 125-foot, Colonial-style edifice. The courthouse, eventually completed for $119,882, featured a beautiful rotunda 32 feet in diameter with a balcony and second-floor offices off the balcony. Gutters and roof valleys were made of copper and the building required a million bricks and 5,000 square feet of flooring. A 48-inch bell and one-ton clock were mounted on a roof tower.

Beneath the mansard roof are an elaborate interior octagonal dome and skylight. Pilasters with Ionic capitals separate arched windows on the second story, which is constructed of salmon-colored brick. A mosaic panel to the right of the main entrance names the building committee, architects and contractor.

**Lincoln County**

**County seat: Merrill**
**Current courthouse:**
  **Year built: 1902**
  **Historic status: Listed in the National Register of Historic Places.**

The tower and exterior window decor, opposite page, are prominent features of the Lincoln County Courthouse. A mosaic floor, at right, brightens the rotunda while a stairway, below, displays metal work.

*Lincoln County*

# Manitowoc County

The county seat was at Manitowoc Rapids when the first courthouse, a wood structure, was built in 1840. The building later burned down during a botched escape attempt by a jail inmate.

After Manitowoc became the county seat, a second courthouse was built in 1857. The building later was moved around the block, where it was used as an armory. Constructed in an Italianate style, it was demolished in the 1950s.

The current courthouse opened in 1906. Listed in the National Register of Historic Places, it was designed by Manitowoc architect Christ H. Tegen as a Beaux Arts, Neoclassical "temple of justice." Tegan also designed the Oneida County Courthouse. The Manitowoc courthouse originally had a glass dome that lighted the rotunda, but the dome was covered with stainless steel in 1948 after a severe storm.

The exterior of the three-story structure is of Indiana limestone with the foundation of red limestone. The central roof has a large enclosed cupola surrounded with a balustrade and capped by a high dome and small open cupola. The balustrade and cupola are covered with copper. Inside, a large, square, open lobby is surrounded by balcony corridors on the second and third floors. The central lobby has a monumental cast iron stairway. Cast plaster columns, pilaster capitals and massive third-

**Manitowoc County**

County seat: Manitowoc
Current courthouse
  Year built: 1906
  Historic status: Listed in the National Register of Historic Places.

floor arches also decorate the interior.

The first lawyer and county judge was Jeremiah H. Colby, who arrived in Manitowoc County in 1845. He settled in Wisconsin due to health reasons and to experience the invigorating air of the West. Colby died of tuberculosis in 1853. In 1850, judges earned $1,500 a year.

Edward Salomon came to Manitowoc in 1852 and soon became deputy clerk of the circuit court. He was admitted to the bar in 1854 and later elected lieutenant governor. Salomon became governor in 1862, when then-governor Louis P. Harvey fell overboard and drowned during an inspection trip of Civil War troops serving in the South.

**Lighting, opposite page and at left, is an important feature of the Manitowoc County Courthouse. Above, mural detail on the interior dome.**

# Marathon County

The former Marathon County Courthouse, circa 1950. Photo courtesy of State Historical Society of Wisconsin, ex. coll. M.M. Harrington.

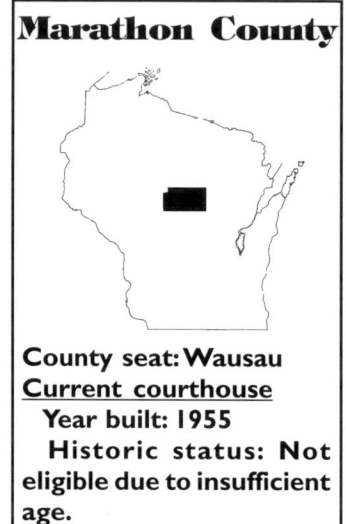

**Marathon County**

**County seat: Wausau**
**Current courthouse**
  **Year built: 1955**
  **Historic status: Not eligible due to insufficient age.**

A small frame building was constructed as Marathon County's first courthouse in 1851. A tiny building housing the clerk's office was built for $98.78.

The second courthouse, constructed in a Greek Revival style, opened in 1868. Marathon County's third courthouse, built in Richardson Romanesque style, served the county from 1892 to 1954. The current courthouse was built in 1955 for $2 million.

One of Marathon County's pioneer lawyers, Louis A. Pradt, came to Wausau in 1872. He became Wausau city attorney in 1890 and, in 1897, was appointed by President William McKinley as assistant U.S. attorney general, a position he held until 1906.

Louis Marchetti was the first municipal judge of Wausau. He became municipal judge in 1877 and was again serving in the post in 1928, when the legislature turned the duties of municipal judges over to the county. Marchetti also served as clerk of the circuit court and as Wausau's mayor from 1901 to 1904.

In 1995, Marathon County Circuit Judge Ann Walsh Bradley was elected to the Wisconsin Supreme Court.

Marinette city and county, part of Michigan until 1836, were named after Queen Marinette, daughter of Wabashish, a Menominee chief. Queen Marinette married Canadian John B. Jacobs and they settled in 1822 at Marinette, where she planted the first orchard. She died in 1863 at the age of 72.

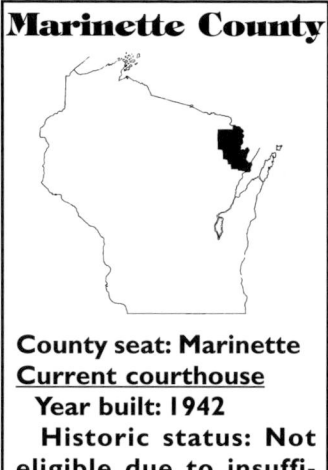

**Marinette County**

County seat: Marinette
**Current courthouse**
 Year built: 1942
 **Historic status: Not eligible due to insufficient age.**

The county clerk was authorized to hire George Clark, a British engineer, to design Marinette County's first courthouse. Clark had designed buildings in Hong Kong, Calcutta and Brazil. The courthouse, based on Clark's plans, was finished in 1879.

Clark's courthouse was razed and a $291,134 courthouse built on approximately the same site in 1941-42. The county's share was $150,000 and federal funds paid the rest. An annex was built in 1992 that is 60 percent the size of the 1942 courthouse.

In a 1906 article by Edward E. Payne, Marinette, the county seat, was called the young Chicago of northern Wisconsin because of the "untiring energy and enterprise of her citizens and a location that permits a tremendous multiplication of enterprises and their profitable pursuit."

Another early factor in Marinette's success was water power from the Menominee River. The population in 1906 was 18,760.

Marinette County was the largest lumber-producing county in the region during the mid-1800s and was part of Oconto County until 1879.

11088.    Marinette County Court House.
Marinette, Wis.

**The Marinette County Courthouse, circa 1905. Photo courtesy of State Historical Society of Wisconsin (postcard collection).**

*Marinette County*

# Marquette County

The Marquette County Courthouse is of simple design but an important community landmark. The state's largest cottonwood tree and a courtroom view are on the opposite page.

P.C. Potter donated an office building in the village of Marquette for use as a courthouse as long as he could be assured that the county seat would remain in the village.

Nine years later, in 1859, the county seat was moved to Montello and the first courthouse was built in 1863. The courthouse was built of stone and brick and featured a second-floor courtroom. The building was replaced in 1918 with the current courthouse on a hill overlooking Lake Montello. The struture is a simple Beaux Arts design but the building is an imposing visual landmark with a strong cornice, projecting pavilion and portico and exterior of locally quarried stone.

An effort was made in 1968 to save the original Montello courthouse as a museum. Young Jim McNamara built a replica, complete with a rooftop cupola encircled by a widow's walk. Pledges of $3,120 were made to save it and among those campaigning to preserve the courthouse was then-Assemblyman Tommy Thompson.

The state's largest tree, a 138-foot cottonwood with a 23.2-foot circumference, grows outside on the courthouse lawn.

**Marquette County**

County seat: Montello
**Current courthouse**
 Year built: 1918
 Historic status: Listed in the National Register of Historic Places.

Marquette County

# Menominee County

Menominee County, which includes the reservation of the Menominee Indians, is Wisconsin's youngest county and the only one without a courthouse. Some court proceedings are heard in neighboring Shawano or Marinette counties and others related to incidents that occur on the reservation are heard in federal court in Milwaukee.

The Menominee Indians, whose name means "wild rice gatherers," are the oldest known continuous residents of Wisconsin. When the 276,400-acre reservation became Wisconsin's 72nd county in 1961, the reservation status was terminated and thousands of acres were bought by white buyers, after many Indian property owners defaulted on their payments.

The reservation and tribal status were restored in 1973, although Menominee remains a Wisconsin county. An 1854 treaty established the reservation at 276,400 acres but it was reduced to 230,400 acres in 1856.

Unemployment traditionally has been high among the Menominees and tribal businesses include a casino, bingo, supermarket, logging camp museum and sawmill.

**Menominee County**

County seat: Keshena
**Current courthouse**
  Year built: n/a
  Historic status: Menominee County has no courthouse.

Menominee Indian Mills.

The sawmill of Menominee Indian Mills at Neopit, circa 1900. Photo courtesy of the State of Wisconsin Historical Society, presented by Charles E. Brown, 1916.

**A statue of Gen. Douglas MacArthur, a Milwaukee native, stands watch over the Milwaukee County Courthouse.**

Befitting Wisconsin's most populous county, the Milwaukee County Courthouse is the most monumental of all Neoclassical courthouses in the state. The three-story structure features an arcade of rounded arches and Corinthian colonades rising several stories and was praised by architectural historian Richard Perrin as the last of important Wisconsin buildings in the classical resurgence. The courthouse occupies an entire block in the central city and looms above neighboring buildings.

The first Milwaukee County courthouse was built in 1836, a year after the county, then a part of Michigan territory, was organized. It was built on the block that now is Cathedral Square, bordered by Kilbourn, Wells, Jackson and Jefferson, on land donated by Solomon Juneau and Morgan Martin. The courthouse and jail cost $5,000.

The county and city soon outgrew the original courthouse and a second courthouse was built in 1873 on Cathedral Square for $650,000.

In 1909, the Milwaukee Metropolitan Park Commission pro-

# Milwaukee County

posed grouping city and county government buildings in a civic center bounded by Ninth, Fourth, Wells and State streets. The plan was endorsed by leading planners of the time, including John Nolen, Frederick Law Olmstead and Werner Hegmann.

Other counties battled over the location of county seats. In Milwaukee County, debate centered on whether the courthouse should be located on the east or west side of the river. The park commission plan called for moving it from the east to west side. Voters approved the west side location in 1920 and the county board appropriated money for a courthouse site. The city issued bonds in 1924, but voters rescinded approval of the west side location the following year. But the land already had been acquired so the city and county forged ahead to begin construction of the civic buildings.

Architect Albert Randolph Ross won a national competition in which thirty-three plans were submitted with Milwaukee architect Alfred Clas as the judge. Seven million dollars was set aside for construction.

**Milwaukee County**

County seat: Milwaukee
**Current courthouse**
 Year built: 1931
 Historic status: Listed in the National Register of Historic Places.

The University of Wisconsin Extension Building was completed in 1928, the first structure in the civic center complex. Kilbourn Avenue was widened and the City-County Public Safety Building was built in 1930 followed by the courthouse in 1931.

Even after construction, controversy surrounding the courthouse continued. Socialist Mayor Dan Hoan and planning director Charles B. Whitehall had spearheaded the drive for construction after a 20-year debate. But architect Frank Lloyd Wright said the building was a 50-year cultural setback for Milwaukee. Despite Wright's criticism, Milwaukee's civic center buildings are viewed today as a pioneer effort at regional planning.

The nation's first all-woman jury in Milwaukee County, 1928. Photo courtesy of State Historical Society of Wisconsin, ex. coll. Judge Charles Aarons, 1958. Neg. WHi (x3) 14455.

## Monroe County

County seat: Sparta
**Current courthouse**
Year built: 1896
Historic status: Listed
in the National Register
of Historic Places.

A $600 courthouse, built in 1855, was used in Monroe County until it was replaced in 1864 by a $20,750 building which housed the courthouse and jail.

The current courthouse was designed by Mifflin E. Bell and completed in 1896. Built of red sandstone from quarries in the Superior area, the courthouse featured a statute of the figure "Justice" that cost $178.50. The stone walk leading to the entrance cost $377. In contrast to

The square central tower adds elegance to the Monroe County Courthouse.

those prices, $700,000 was spent refurbishing the historic courthouse in 1996.

The stately three-story building was designed in Richardson Romanesque style on a public square. It had a hipped-roof attic crowned by a square central tower with open oriels and round turrets. The original slate roof was replaced by asbestos tile in 1929 but the tile roof was deterio-

rated, leaking and covered with lichens by the 1990s. The original slate roof lasted only 30 years because it was damaged by lack of insulation, causing ice dams to form at the bottom edges. The original gutter system also was deteriorated.

The refurbishing project restored

Dave Oswald, below, fits the repaired face section on Lady Justice, a 104-year-old statue. Oswald also constructed the Big Muskie near Hayward. At right, Clerk of Courts Carol Thorsen climbs stairs.

# Monroe County

the slate roof and copper gutters. Forty-two arched windows also were replaced. Ornamental metal cornice work, which had been eaten away, was refabricated. Four deteriorated capitals and an entry portico were replaced with Indiana limestone and the balustrade was returned to the portico roof after a 50-year absence.

## Oconto County

**County seat: Oconto**
**Current courthouse**
  **Year built: 1891, 1907**
  **Historic status: Listed**
**in the National Register**
**of Historic Places.**

The county's first courthouse burned down in 1891. Designed by Rau & Kirsch, the second Oconto County courthouse was built the same year for $50,000.

Described as a gabled pavilion of blonde brick, the courthouse featured a clock tower and cupola with a statue of Lady Justice balancing her scales on top. Below the sharp peak of the center pavilion was an inset terra cotta plaque displaying the log and fish — symbols of the local

*Oconto County*

economy.

In 1907, fire destroyed the upper level but it was rebuilt in Neoclassical style with a larger cupola, additional dormers and red roof tiles. A low-slung jail annex was added to the east side in 1960. An office wing was added on the west side in 1977. The three-story building on the east side now houses the courtroom, jail and offices.

In 1871, butcher Louie Nohr fired into a throng of drunken revelers, wounding young Joseph Ruckle. Nohr was arrested but an angry mob dragged him from his cell and lynched him from an oak tree. Twenty years later, in a symbolic replacement of mob justice by civilized justice, the second Oconto County Courthouse was erected on the site of the lynching.

**Ted Rockwell watches the clocks at the Oconto County Courthouse.**

Christ H. Tegan of Manitowoc was hired in 1908 to design a courthouse that would replace the frame building that had served as the Oneida County Courthouse since 1887. A stone, concrete and metal building was completed in 1910.

A highlight of the courthouse were a pair of murals painted in 1919 by F. Biberstein on facing third-floor walls. One mural depicted lumbermen rolling on and directing floating logs down the river. The other was a romanticized depiction of three Indians drying and stretching skins in front of their tepees. A smaller mural of a hodag, a mythical monster, decorated the west hall. The murals were commissioned by Conrad Schmitt of Milwaukee, who was given $5,000 in 1919 to decorate the courthouse.

The courthouse, which was listed on the National Register of Historic Places in 1981, was built of gray limestone with towering Ionic columns and perfect Neoclassical symmetry. The courthouse is identical in design to courthouses in Grant and Manitowoc counties.

Ryckman & Sons Co. of Kalamazoo, Mich. was hired to build the courthouse for $96,500 just three years after a fire destroyed most of Rhinelander's north side.

The original frame courthouse was relocated to Baird Avenue, where it was converted for use by

**Oneida County**

**County seat: Rhine-lander**
**Current courthouse**
  Year built: 1910
  Historic status: Listed in the National Register of Historic Places.

**Oneida County**

**Oneida County**

a teacher's college.

When a severe windstorm damaged the courthouse exterior in 1964, some people said the dome should be replaced with a flat roof. But the dome was repaired instead by Eric Friis. In 1987, each half of the dome was removed and repaired in Minnesota. In 1991, the refurbishing was completed and the courthouse was restored to its original beauty.

In 1933, Oneida County passed the first zoning ordinance in the nation.

**The Hodag mural, below, is a focal point. Chandeliers, above, light the courtroom, while a wide stairway sweeps down below the dome, at right.**

Before 1849, citizens of Outagamie County travelled to Green Bay for legal services. Outagamie County's first courthouse was established in the residence of R.P. Edgerton of Appleton.

When the county board met in 1851, Grand Chute was the county seat. But A.A. Lawrence donated a block in Appleton for a courthouse and work began in late 1852. But the original builders opted out of the contract and the courthouse, a 60-foot-square frame building painted white with clapboard siding, wasn't completed until two years later. The county was given a deed for the land with a stipulation that if the courthouse ever moved, the land would revert to its original owners.

In 1855, the county board voted to clear the courthouse square and erect a fence. The sum of $1,200 was appropriated for a fireproof records section.

An early case involved a lawsuit brought by Hermaneque St. Marie against Ephraim St. Louis. St. Marie claimed that St. Louis owed him $70 for a cream-colored mare he had sold to the defendant. But St. Louis filed a counterclaim for $72.85. The judge awarded St. Marie $2.25 plus costs.

Businessmen clamored for a new courthouse in 1867 but the board didn't buy the idea. In 1869, repairs were ordered on the old courthouse.

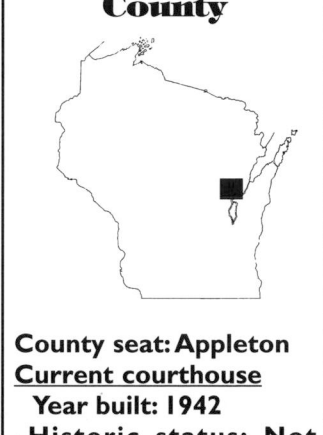

## Outagamie County

**County seat: Appleton**
**Current courthouse**
 **Year built: 1942**
 **Historic status: Not eligible due to insufficient age.**

In 1878, county officials tried to clear up the deed and move the courthouse to downtown Appleton but they failed. A newspaper editorial described the poor condition:

"The courthouse is rotting down and not one in fifty desires to see a new one located where only private residences should be found."

**The Outagamie County Courthouse, circa 1905. Photo courtesy of Ann Waidelich.**

Two years later, the board finally voted to build a new $45,000 courthouse. The architect was H.C. Koch & Co. of Milwaukee and Daniel Stephens of Madison was hired as general contractor. The new courthouse was occupied in 1882.

The county installed an unusual configuration of rotary jail cells in 1887 that were designed by the Rotary Jail Co. of Chicago. Eight cells were arranged in a circle. They were mounted on a turnstile that could be revolved by turning a lever. Revolving the cells would allow the jailer to bring a particular cell to a single entrance. Eleven years later, inmates were moved to a workhouse when the rotary jail was deemed unsafe, especially if a fire were to break out and inmates couldn't be evacuated quickly. A new jail was built in 1905 for $15,000.

By 1942, the courthouse was considered a fire trap and too small. The jail was demolished and a new $550,000 courthouse was completed. Raymond N. LeVee was the architect and Hoffman Construction Co. of Appleton was the contractor. The 215-room structure was built of Indiana limestone with wood paneling, asphalt and rubber tiled floors and two elevators. The courthouse also featured then-modern "skeleton clocks" with markings on the dial instead of numbers.

**Outagamie County**

Ozaukee County

The first courthouse, a three-story brick structure, was built in 1854 at Port Washington for $12,000. The first floor was used as a jail and living quarters for the jailer. Offices were on the second floor and a courtroom on the third floor. In 1867, a fireproof building was erected adjacent to the courthouse for $6,000 to house the register of deeds and other county offices.

**Ozaukee County**

County seat: Port Washington
__Historic courthouse__
   Year built: 1902
   Historic status: Listed in the National Register of Historic Places.

In 1899, the county board declared the first courthouse unsafe and solicited bids for a new one. Initial bids were over $50,000, which county officials considered too high, so new bids were solicited. The final cost of the new courthouse, including furnishings was $58,014.

During its first year of use, the eagle on the courthouse tower was struck by lightning and replaced for a cost of $252.

By 1959, county government began to outgrow the turn-of-the-century courthouse. A 1965 study recommended that a courthouse annex be constructed between the existing courthouse and jail. A $2.2 million bond issue was authorized to finance construction, which was completed in 1969.

In 1991, construction began on a $16 million justice center to house the jail, sheriff and related departments. The old courthouse and annex were remodeled with a fire alarm system and refinished woodwork, along with new carpeting and vinyl wall coverings. The remodeling project cost $2.8 million.

A ceiling mural is displayed above. A new Ozaukee County Courthouse was built in 1991, but the old courthouse, opposite page, survives as a historic landmark.

**Ozaukee County**

# Pepin County

**County seat: Durand**
**Historic courthouse**
 Year built: 1874
 Historic status: Listed
in the **National Register**
of **Historic Places.**

Court in Pepin County is held in a former surgery room in an old hospital. The agricultural services office is in the old hospital laundry while the human services department occupies the maternity ward. The remodeled hospital has been used as a courthouse since 1984.

Before that, Pepin County used one of the last remaining wooden courthouses in the state. The original courthouse, was built for $7,000 in 1874 in Greek Revival style. The courthouse,

**Pepin County's historic courthouse, one of Wisconsin's last remaining wooden courthouses, now is a museum.**

built after a long battle between Durand and Arkansaw over which community would become the county seat, is considered responsible for Durand's survival.

In 1859, voters rejected moving the county seat from Pepin to Durand by three votes. Another referendum to move the county seat passed 429-327 three years later. The decision was challenged in court but the vote was upheld. In 1881, voters approved moving the county seat to Arkansaw and rejected a move back to Durand the following year.

After those two votes, it looked like Arkansaw would become the county seat. But in 1886, voters approved Durand as the county seat.

The first county judge was S.S.N. Fuller and another early judge was H.L. Humphrey, who was elected to Congress in 1877. Egbert B. Bundy became judge in 1877 after a bitter political battle and held the post for 20 years.

An early case was the murder of Ira Bradley Wheeler, who lived on the banks of the Chippewa River two miles west of Pepin Village with his wife, Margaret, their two children and Wheeler's business partner, James E. Carter. Wheeler and Carter supplied fuel for steam boats.

On March 24, 1866, the family was prepared to go to Carter's sister's home to play cards when Mrs. Wheeler began criticizing her husband for cheating at cards. A bitter quarrel erupted and Wheeler and Carter came to blows. Wheeler was killed in the struggle. Carter and Mrs. Wheeler dropped his body, along with his horse and sleigh, through a hole in the river ice.

When the ice melted and Wheeler's body was found, an inquest determined he died from a blow to the head probably inflicted with a hatchet or gun barrel. Carter and Mrs. Wheeler were taken to La Crosse County for trial. Carter confessed during the trial that he killed Wheeler after Wheeler attacked him with a club. The jury believed he was protecting Mrs. Wheeler and found both guilty. They were sentenced to life in prison.

Mrs. Wheeler appealed her conviction to the Supreme Court. She was released but quickly arrested again. She fled with a former lover and the law didn't pursue her. When Carter was pa-

Vera Slabey, director of the Old Courthouse Museum, opens a cell door.

roled in 1874, he said Mrs. Wheeler had struck the fatal hatchet blow. Carter married and became a foreman at a lumber mill.

Durand gained the reputation of "a hanging town" after the 1881 lynching of Ed Maxwell, alias Ed Williams, one of the last lynchings in the state. Maxwell, who had stolen a couple of horses in Illinois with his brother, fatally shot ex-sheriff Charles G. Coleman and his brother, Deputy Milton Coleman, as they tried to arrest him. Maxwell later was arrested for the murders and, on the way back from a court hearing before Judge W.B. Dyer, members of a mob tackled deputies, threw a noose around Maxwell's neck and hung him 30 feet in the air from an oak tree outside the courthouse.

Pierce County

**A hexagonal dome is a unique feature of the Pierce County Courthouse.**

Pierce County's first settlement was in 1827 at the junction of the St. Croix and Mississippi rivers in Prescott, although the area had been explored in the 1670s by Father Louis Hennepin and French fur traders.

The county was created in 1853 and logging soon came to the area, although dairy farming ultimately became the most important economic activity with wheat, corn and oats as the principal crops. Ready river transportation made it easy for farmers to bring their crops to market.

The first county seat was at Prescott but was moved after an 1861 referendum to Ellsworth, one of the first population centers and a more central location. The county soon outgrew its first courthouse and a second one was built in 1879. It was replaced by the current courthouse in 1905.

The current courthouse, built on a hillside facing a commercial area, shows both simple Neoclassical and Beaux

Arts characteristics. It features a hexagonal dome with alternating, multi-pane windows; Ionic columns; and a rusticated red sandstone raised basement. The main entrance is centered in a pedimented parapet in the center pavilion. Sculpted figures and a crest over the doorway represent the

## Pierce County

County seat: Ellsworth
**Current courthouse**
Year built: 1905
Historic status: Listed in the National Register of Historic Places.

state seal.

Glass-globed wall sconces, dressed limestone walls and marble wainscoting highlight the interior. Outdoor scenes painted in shades of green and gray decorate the faces of the dome.

A three-story brick stair tower in a mauve color was added in 1970 on the east end of the building. More recently, the county spent $135,000 to repair the dome when it developed leaks, instead of removing it at lower cost.

Fireproof safes became a standard feature of many courthouses after several fires destroyed county records during the late 19th Century.

Polk County

Polk County, originally part of Crawford County, was created from portions of Barron, Chippewa and Ashland counties in 1853. The county was named after James K. Polk, the nation's eleventh president.

The first county seat was at St. Croix Falls and court was convened in a schoolhouse. The first county board met in Fretland's building in Oseola Mills. Issac Fretland was the county's first attorney and later became clerk of the circuit court. Issac W. Hale was the first county judge.

An 1853 referendum moved the county seat to Osceola where, a decade later, the county records were stolen. They weren't recovered and Polk County's early history is sparse.

Many Civil War veterans claimed land in Polk County and a farm owned by William Blanding known as "Jerusalem" was a popular 19th Century resort, where baseball games and picnics often were held.

Balsam Lake, which became the county seat in 1898, was organized in 1870. Polk County's historic courthouse was built in 1899, the first at Balsam Lake, and now is occupied by the Polk County Historical Museum. Construction of the courthouse, jail and a sheriff's residence were financed through the sale of $25,000 in bonds. Architects Orff &

**Polk County**

County seat: Balsam Lake
**Historic courthouse**
  Year built: 1899
  Historic status: Listed in the National Register of Historic Places.

Guilbert of Minneapolis designed the building with a Victorian Era colorism and Richardsonian Romanesque references.

The county seat rivalry was still smoldering in 1899 and the *Polk County Press* in Osceola didn't report on construction of the Balsam Lake courthouse. A new courthouse was built in 1975 and the former sheriff's residence and jail was recently torn down to provide a housing site.

A sixty-foot-square building, Polk County's historic courthouse is two stories with the exterior of red pressed brick, an attic under a hipped roof and a basement for storage and utilities. It features a central tower and four corner towers. The main entrance is recessed between brick columns with an inscription stone that reads "18 Polk County 98" overhead.

The interior was remodeled in 1965, leaving only remnants of the original courthouse. A pediment supported by pairs of Doric columns is behind the judge's bench.

**Lighting detail is shown above while an exterior view is on the opposite page.**

*Polk County*

Portage County

William Dunston was awarded a $1,950 contract in 1845 to build Portage County's first courthouse in Plover. Dunston quit the job but was ordered to start again. By 1849, the courthouse was completed but the county board threatened to withhold payment unless Dunston cleaned up wood shavings and debris, finished hanging the doors and installed locks.

**Portage County**

County seat: Stevens Point
Current courthouse
  Year built: 1959
  Historic status: Not eligible due to insufficient age.

The former Portage County Courthouse, circa 1910. Photo courtesy of State Historical Society of Wisconsin (postcard collection).

The sheriff swept up the shavings and bought lights for the courthouse. But vandals smashed the windows and people began stealing various items. In 1850, Miner Strope was ordered to return a piece of stove pipe he had stolen from the courthouse. Strope later served three terms as county judge and became the first president of the Portage County Bar Association.

Stevens Point won a bitter struggle with Plover over location of the county seat. One referendum was thrown out after the Wisconsin Supreme Court decided that non-residents had voted. The court ordered another referendum and, in 1869, Stevens Point won by a slim margin.

In 1867, $10,000 was set aside for a courthouse on a public square in the new county seat of Stevens Point. But that courthouse wasn't built because of the ongoing county seat dispute. Three years later, the county's second courthouse was constructed at Stevens Point.

That courthouse was replaced in 1959 with a city-county building on the same site. Architect for the $1.06-million structure was Ray R. Gauger & Co. and Orville Madsen & Sons Inc. of St. Paul was the general contractor.

An early case was the murder of Sheriff Baker in a squabble over the estate of Luther Hatchett, who died in 1861 while serving in Congress. Amos Cartwright was Hatchett's partner in a sawmill. In 1856, Hatchett sold his interest to Cartwright. After Hatchett died, there were suits and countersuits over his estate until 1868, when Amos Cartwright and his brother seized a house they believed was rightfully theirs. They threatened to shoot the sheriff if he tried to evict them. As the sheriff and four deputies passed through the front gate to serve the papers, the Cartwrights opened fire, killing Baker and wounding Deputy David Cameron.

The murderers escaped but were recaptured. While they were held in jail, a party of armed, masked men broke in, dragged the Cartwright brothers outside and lynched them.

Phillips was platted in 1876 by the Wisconsin Central Railroad and named in honor of Elijah Phillips, the railroad's general manager.

The first Price County courthouse, a two-story frame building with a tower, was erected in 1880. Another courthouse of brick and stone replaced it. A third courthouse was built in 1976.

The first jail was built in 1880 for $665 but it burned in an 1895 fire. The second jail was built that year for $13,320.

Willis Hand, who later became a county judge, prosecuted one of the county's first murder cases against Mitch Gereau, the keeper of a house of prostitution. Gereau was acquitted of the murder of Jack Ryan after claiming he fired the fatal shot in self-defense.

The area's houses of prostitution served the needs of 2,000 to 4,000 loggers during the late nineteenth century.

## Price County

County seat: Phillips
Current courthouse
  Year built: 1976
  Historic status: Not eligible due to insufficient age.

Price County Jail, Phillips, Wis.

The Price County Jail, above, and courthouse, below, both circa 1910. Photos courtesy of State Historical Society of Wisconsin. Jail photo: postcard collection; courthouse photo: neg. WHi C741 1360.

Court House
Phillips, Wis.  T-34.

**Price County**

# Racine County

A small, white frame building became Racine County's first courthouse in 1842, three years after the county was created. The first courthouse was built on Racine's west side but the second courthouse, completed in 1876, was built downtown at Main and Sixth streets.

Racine County's surviving historic courthouse, an imposing block structure, opened in 1931 on the site of Wisconsin's first high school. It opened the same week as a new city hall and new post office. A law enforcement center was built in 1982.

The county's first lawsuit grew out of a squirrel hunt. Two teams competed to find out which team could collect the most heads of animal prey. According to the rules, they were allowed to acquire the heads by any means. Marshall Strong, one of the competitors, had heard of a live wolf that someone was keeping in Chicago and he went to get it. On the way back, he stopped at Willis' tavern on the Chicago Stage Road, where he encountered a band of rowdy sailors. One of the sailors hit the wolf with a gin bottle and killed it.

Strong sued Captain Smith, the sailor, for killing the wolf. Strong won the suit and was awarded six cents plus costs. He also won the animal contest by bringing a collection of muskrat noses back from Milwaukee.

## Racine County

**County seat: Racine**
**Current courthouse**
**Year built: 1931**
**Historic status: Listed in the National Register of Historic Places.**

The engraving of a worker, above, is on an elevator door while the stone carving, at left, appears at the west entrance. The monolithic courthouse rises into the sky on the opposite page.

# Richland County

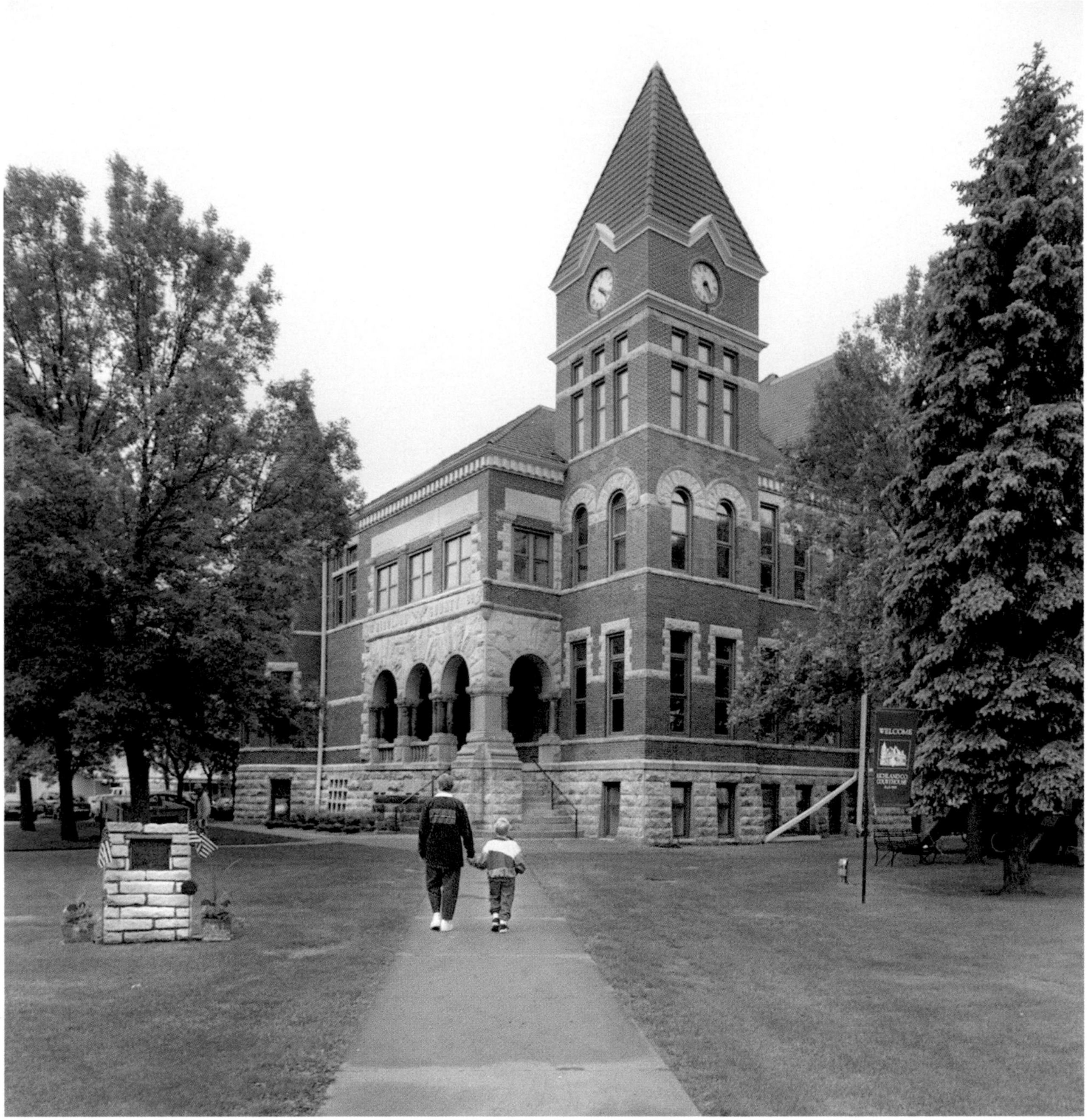

**Richland County**

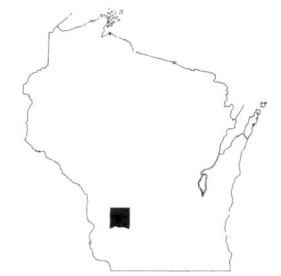

**County seat: Richland Center**
**<u>Current courthouse</u>**
**Year built: 1890, 1937, 1953**
**Historic status: Not eligible due to loss of integrity.**

Monongahela, a small Indian town, was selected as the first county seat but an 1851 referendum moved the county seat to Richland Center. Ira Haseltine, the founder of Richland Center, offered land for a courthouse and jail and, in 1856, Haseltine bid $1,325 to build the courthouse.

The "little courthouse," a two-story frame building with a cupola and courtroom on the second floor, was completed in 1857 and a jail was built of elm logs.

The first courthouse burned in 1860 after a fire was ignited by sparks from a cigar.

Haseltine got another contract in 1860 to build a second courthouse. This 28-foot by 38-foot courthouse had a courtroom on the first floor and brick flooring to guard against another fire. But county officials didn't like the second courthouse and, in 1867, a judge temporarily moved proceedings to another location.

But it wasn't until 1890 that Richland County's third courthouse was ready for occupancy.

The courthouse was refurbished in 1937 as part of a WPA (Works Progress Administration) project. Old varnish was removed and walls and ceilings were painted. In 1953, plans were made to remove the cupola, clock tower and steep gables. Instead, an electronic clock was installed.

One of Richland County's most famous murder cases was the murder of Ella Maly by Rose Zoldoski. A milliner and housekeeper for Dr. G.R. Mitchell, Zoldoski hosted a party at Mitchell's house on Jan. 8, 1891, and invited Elly Maly and her sister, Lilly. Rose gave Elly a piece of candy and Elly ate it on the way home. When Elly said the candy tasted bitter, Lilly figured the taste was due to burnt chocolate. But Elly had a convulsion on the way and several more during the night before she died the next day.

At first, doctors believed that Elly's death was caused by urine poisoning. Later, they determined it was caused by strychnine in the candy. An examination of other pieces of candy in Elly's pocket turned up no poison.

But Dr. Mitchell's wife also had died of convulsions and it turned that Rose Zoldoski was infatuated with the doctor and apparently jealous of Elly Maly. When the wife's body was exhumed, strychnine also was found in her remains. Zoldoski was sentenced to life in prison but was pardoned by the governor in 1896.

**Although the Richland County Courthouse has undergone considerable remodeling, historic aspects such as the columns above and the striking exterior on the opposite page remain.**

**Richland County**

**Rock County**

Rock County's courthouse park in Janesville, circa 1910. Photo courtesy of State Historical Society of Wisconsin.

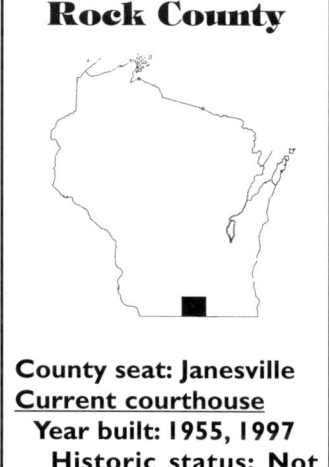

**Rock County**

County seat: Janesville
**Current courthouse**
**Year built: 1955, 1997**
**Historic status: Not eligible due to insufficient age.**

Rock County's first courthouse and a log jail were occupied in 1842. The courthouse burned in 1859 and was rebuilt a decade later for $124,672. Early in the twentieth century, a smaller courthouse was built at Beloit.

In 1856, Janesville had eight thousand people, five grist mills, five livery stables, a carriage factory, a woolen factory and three newspapers. Wheat farmers from New York were attracted to the fertile Rock County soil.

The first circuit judge serving Rock and other southwestern counties was Edward V. Whiton, who later became Wisconsin's first chief justice of the Supreme Court. He also served in the territorial legislature and, according to one account, "Judge Whiton was elected largely because he had great personal magnetism and because he had won support of influential groups in the county."

In the early 1950s, the county board was debating whether to build a new courthouse and whether it should be in Janesville or Beloit. The debate apparently grew too spirited for the old courthouse's county board chamber because suddenly a loud cracking noise was heard and a 1.5-inch-deep crack appeared in the ceiling. The meeting ended, the courthouse was evacuated and the ceiling was shored up with wooden posts.

The ceiling crack quickly settled the courthouse debate and a new courthouse was completed in 1955. An addition was built on the site of the old courthouse in 1997.

In 1885, the city of Flambeau Mills, which eventually became Ladysmith, was laid out by railroad surveyors from the Sault St. Marie Land & Improvement Co. Earlier, the town had been called Crooked Rapids. A 1895 railroad timetable listed the town simply as Flambeau.

The name was changed to Warner in 1898 to honor a stockholder in the Soo Line Railroad. At the turn of the century, Warner had a population of 100.

But Warner soon would experience a population boom. Charles R. Smith, president of Menasha Wooden Ware Inc., wanted to build a branch plant at Warner. He also planned to marry Isabel Bacon Rogers, a Neenah socialite. As an incentive for Smith to build the plant, Warner residents changed the name to Ladysmith to honor his fiancé. The city of Ladysmith, South Africa, where the British were fighting the Boers in the Boer War, also was in the news at the time.

**Rusk County**

County seat: Ladysmith
Current courthouse
  Year built: 1902
  Historic status: Not eligible due to loss of integrity.

The name of Rusk County was as difficult to come by as Ladysmith. On May 9, 1901, Gates County was created and Ladysmith became the county seat. The new county was formed after grumbling that Chippewa Falls was too far to travel for court and county business. Some wanted to name the new county after former Gov. Jeremiah Rusk but Rusk's son fought against the county's formation and it was named instead after James L. Gates, a land dealer.

In 1902, the $25,000 Gates County courthouse was completed and a ball was held in June in the new building. The courthouse featured a cupola and $2,000 was spent on furnishings. A year earlier, western county residents, angered that Ladysmith had been designated the county seat, asked for an injunction prohibiting courthouse construction but the injunction was dissolved by a circuit judge. The residents appealed to the Wisconsin Supreme Court, which upheld the judge's ruling.

In 1905, the county's name was changed to Rusk County because Gates had failed to pay $10,000 he had promised to the county for naming it after him. Gates, who had a somewhat unscrupulous reputation, tried to contest the action but failed. The *Gates County Journal* waited until November to change its name to the *Rusk County Journal*. Editor Del Crandall said he wanted to make sure the Rusk County name would stick.

**The original Rusk County Courthouse. Photo courtesy of Mary Bloedow.**

Rusk County

# St. Croix County

The first circuit court was established at Dakotah in 1840 but, when the western part of St. Croix County was given to Minnesota in 1848, the action left the county seat in the other state. Land was donated the same year by Phil Aldrich for a new county building in Hudson.

The county was named for Monsieur St. Croix, a seventeenth century explorer who drowned at the mouth of the river.

In 1849, Hudson was a bustling city and it was predicted that the city would become much larger than St. Paul due to better river navigation. In 1851, the county board appropriated $350 to build a county jail. Ammah Andrews was awarded a $14,300 contract in 1856 to build a courthouse. An elegant two-story courthouse with Ionic columns and a cupola was completed for $20,045 the following year.

At the turn of the century, residents fought to move the county seat to a more central location. In 1900, a new $50,000 courthouse was built in Richardson Romanesque style was built on Third Street in Hudson. Richardson Romanesque was a style based on the work of architect Henry Richards.

The courthouse, which featured massive archways, was built of heavy rough hewn stone by the Andrew brothers on the site of the 1857 courthouse.

A courthouse annex was built in 1966 for $725,000. When a $12.6-million government cen-

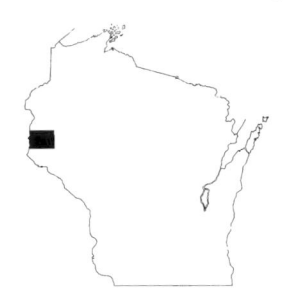

**St. Croix County**

**County seat: Hudson**
**Historic courthouse**
  **Year built: 1900**
  **Historic status: Listed in the National Register of Historic Places.**

ter was completed in 1993, the 1966 courthouse was sold to the city for use as a library and offices. The 1900 courthouse was sold to condominium developer David Tank. The 139,000-square-foot government center houses 160 employees and a 128-inmate jail. It also has parking for 250 cars.

One of the first cases involved a man who was severely beaten. The man was arrested and the complaining witness showed up with five gallons of whiskey.

A six-man jury was empaneled and the arrested man was given the choice of going to jail in Prairie du Chien or paying $300 plus court costs.

But the prisoner had no money and it would cost $100 to send him to Prairie du Chien, so bail was set at $300 and he was ordered to keep the peace for a year. The complaining witness and the justice of the peace put up the man's bail.

**St. Croix County's 1900 courthouse now is privately owned. The south entrance is at right while an exterior view is on the opposite page.**

St. Croix County

**Sauk County**

Sauk County's first courthouse in Baraboo was built on the north side of the square in 1848. The two-story building housed a courtroom that also was used for church services, a classroom and as a dance hall. One time, a church group showed up to use the courtroom at the same time as a group of dancers. The situation was resolved when the music began, people began dancing and the church group left. The courthouse eventually was turned into a saloon and burned down in 1857.

Before 1846, the county seat was at Prairie du Sac. On one occasion, court proceedings were interrupted by a man who burst in shouting, "Bear in the village! Bear in the village!" Everyone scurried outside to help capture the bear, which provided a feast for the villagers. Among the bear catchers was Count Agoston Haraszthy, who platted the village of Prairie du Sac.

In 1850, Reedsburg residents fought to move the county seat to their community. In what became known as the Reedsburg War, residents blocked the dam so logs couldn't flow down the river and the U.S. marshal was called in to open the dam. A referendum in 1852 kept the county seat at Baraboo.

The county's first Baraboo courthouse, a two-story wooden structure, was built in 1848. When that courthouse burned down in 1857, P.A. Bassett was awarded a $5,000 contract to build a 40-foot

**Sauk County**

County seat: Baraboo
**Current courthouse**
  Year built: 1906
  Historic status: Listed in the National Register of Historic Places.

by 20-foot brick courthouse and a hexagonal jail. Later, Frederick Baringer was given a $6,000 contract to build an addition.

The brick courthouse burned down on July 4, 1904, but a month earlier, the county board had appropriated $100,000 for a new courthouse. T.C. McCarthy of Madison was named general contractor with a bid of $83,384. The architect was Ferry & Clas of Milwaukee.

An unusual aspect of the 1906 courthouse was that it had two cornerstones. One cornerstone was laid by the county and another by Charles Hirschinger. The courthouse, built of warm gray Indiana limestone, featured Ionic pilasters on the front with cornices that harmonize with the design. The roof was of green glazed terra cotta with copper ridges and angles. The cupola was covered with copper and the Latin word "Lex" was inscribed on the freize of the main cornice. Inside were a two-story courtroom and a staircase hall of darkish red Tennessee marble.

In 1915, part of the upper tower was rebuilt so bells could be installed. The courthouse was expanded and rededicated in 1989, then remodeled in 1996.

An early criminal case involved Judson Baxter and William H. Reynolds who arrived in Reedburg on a lumber wagon and were accused of paying their hotel bill with bogus coin.

**Kids, above, play on the cannon on the courthouse lawn. A courtroom, above right, was restored with modern chairs. A marble stairway, lower right, leads to the second floor.**

**Sauk County**

**Sawyer County**

Sawyer County was named for Philetus Sawyer of Oshkosh. During the mid-19th Century, Sawyer rose from a mill hand and woodsman to become a prosperous lumber manufacturer and land speculator. He also served in Congress for a decade before 1875.

The county was created in 1883 from parts of Chippewa and Ashland counties. Chippewa County was paid $96,000 for land turned over to Sawyer County.

The first courthouse was built of pine clapboard in 1884. Before the courthouse was built, the county's cases were heard in Ashland. Land was bought for the courthouse for $1,000 in December 1883. A committee met the following April to plan the building and, in July, N.B. Rundle was awarded an $18,000 construction contract. The building opened in 1885.

Hayward, the county seat, was named for Anthony Judson Hayward, who established a sawmill in the area. He also served as the first chairman of the three-member county board from 1883 to 1886.

In 1962, the courthouse was razed to make room for a new courthouse on the same site. A clerk of courts wing was added in 1992 and a health and human services wing in 1998.

During the 1920s and 1930s, gangsters from Chicago often vacationed in Sawyer County. When they were vacationing, they mostly left their violent criminal behavior behind. Joe Saltis once was arrested while fly fishing. Al Capone also had a place that is preserved today as "The Hideout." Al's brother, Ralph Capone, had a reputation as an upstanding citizen who contributed to the community.

The county's most famous case, however, was that of John Dietz during the early years of the twentieth century. Angered over back wages he claimed were owed him by a logging company, Dietz blocked a spring logging drive on the Thornapple River, which was on his property. Dietz ultimately was arrested after a long standoff of several years and a gun battle at his home. By this time, he had become a national folk hero for taking a stand against the government and wealthy logging interests.

**Sawyer County**

**County seat: Hayward**
**Current courthouse**
  Year built: 1962
  Historic status: Not eligible due to insufficient age.

**The former Sawyer County Courthouse, circa 1905-1910. Photo courtesy of Ann Waidelich.**

Capt. Elias Murray was Shawano County's first white settler. He was appointed superintendent of the Indians of the Northwest Territory by President Tyler in 1850 and charged with moving the Menominee tribe to the reservation.

The county was formed in 1853 and when the first Fourth of July celebration was held in the following

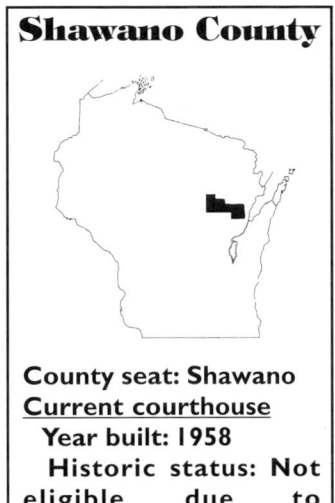

**Shawano County**

County seat: Shawano
Current courthouse
   Year built: 1958
   Historic status: Not eligible due to insufficient age.

The former Shawano County Courthouse peeks through the trees in this circa 1908 photo, courtesy of State Historical Society of Wisconsin.

year, all six Shawano families attended. The first election of county officers was held at the home of Charles D. Westcott. Shawano's first mayor was D.H. Pulcifer and early lawyers included Joseph Maurer, G.W. Latta, D.P. Andrews, K.M. Phillips and E.L. Farnsworth.

In 1864, the county name was changed from "Shaw-an-aw," a Menominee term meaning "to the south." Indians named the area after finding an abundance of wild rice.

Shawano County's second courthouse and jail

were built for $17,000 by J. L. Whitehouse in 1883. Charles Westcott helped with courthouse planning. Fire destroyed a portion of Main Street in 1890 but the courthouse was spared. A jail was built on the southwest corner of the courthouse block in 1901 and used until a courthouse and jail for 38 prisoners were built in 1956.

When the new courthouse opened in 1958, the old courthouse was gone but three elm trees planted in 1884 on the courthouse square survived.

**Shawano County**

# Sheboygan County

A.L. Weeks designed Sheboygan County's third courthouse in 1868 and his son, W.C. Weeks of Sheboygan, designed the fourth one in 1934.

The first court was held in 1846 at the home of R.P. Harriman and was moved to a school-house the following year. A wooden structure was built in 1851 with a court-room on the second floor and a jail on the first floor. On New Year's

**Sheboygan County**

**County seat: Sheboygan**
**Current courthouse**
 **Year built: 1934**
 **Historic status: Listed in the National Register of Historic Places.**

Day 1860, in 14-below-zero temperatures, fire destroyed the courthouse along with many county records and papers.

A brick courthouse with 20-inch-thick walls, large arched doorways and floor-to-ceiling windows protected by heavy iron screens was quickly erected after the fire. The building later was converted to a dwelling.

The Weeks-designed courthouse of 1868 returned the building to its original site of Sixth Street and Center Avenue. The $65,000 building was a Victorian structure of gray brick with a clock and bell tower. It had eight chimneys and was heated with wood stoves. Weeks had moved to Sheboygan from Martha's Vineyard in 1848.

In 1893, $46,000 was allocated for a new jail and fireproof records vaults. During the 1920s, some residents wanted to build a new courthouse at Fountain Park but the land originally had been dedicated only for park purposes.

The 1934 courthouse, designed by the younger Weeks, was in Art Deco style and built of gray granite and Indiana limestone. The main lobbies and stairways were paneled floor to ceiling with Etowah pink Georgia marble. The courthouse, which cost $575,000 including the grounds and furnishings, featured terrazzo floors with brass dividing strips and ornamental aluminum radiator grills in the main lobby. The courthouse originally had two courtrooms, each two stories high.

When the 1868 courthouse was demolished in 1934, the courthouse clock was installed in the Franklin School tower. In 1956, a courthouse annex was built to house the municipal court and an $868,594 remodeling project in 1967 added an intermediate floor with two additional courtrooms.

**A lion's head, top, stands watch while the interior, above, is softly lit. Geometric lines, opposite page, decorate an elevator door and the courthouse's block style is evident in an exterior view.**

*Sheboygan County*

Taylor County

A bitter battle over courthouse siting in 1875 resulted in construction of two Taylor County courthouses on opposite sides of town.

When the county board advertised for courthouse bids, two local businessmen offered five acres on the west side of the railroad tracks and the Wisconsin Central Railroad Co. offered land on the east side. The board accepted the railroad's offer and residents circulated a petition favoring the other site.

A special election was held on Oct. 15, 1875, and voters favored the west side site by a margin of 264-80. The election also authorized spending $6,000 for the new courthouse. A peoples' building committee formed, but the county officials said they would use the building committee's plans only if the courthouse were built on the east side railroad property.

The county board awarded a $5,200 contract for the east side courthouse and the peoples' committee began putting up their own courthouse on the west side. The peoples' committee appealed to the legislature but bills failed to legalize their courthouse.

"The fight caused so much hard feelings that it made enemies of former friends for a generation," a newspaper reported.

The east side courthouse was completed in

**Taylor County**

County seat: Medford
<u>Current courthouse</u>
  Year built: 1914
  Historic status: Listed in the National Register of Historic Places.

1876 but officials didn't move in for a year due to the dispute. The west side courthouse stood empty for several years and eventually was converted into a store and a residence later occupied by Judge Clinton Extor.

But the county still didn't have a jail. Two men were brought from Clark County to face trial for burning a building in Taylor. When one was found guilty and the other innocent, they had to be taken to a blacksmith shop to have their chains cut off.

**Mary Ann Knopp, above, is behind bars in the treasurer's office. An exterior view is on the opposite page.**

Taylor County

**Taylor County**

Mike Hurley, the first constable, arrested a man for stealing a pair of boots from Dodge & Healy's store. Because there was no jail, Hurley brought the prisoner to his room. By morning, the prisoner had disappeared with Hurley's boots, watch, money and pants.

The county eventually built a jail but an 1892 fire destroyed it along with the sheriff's residence.

A $57,203 contract was awarded in 1913 to build a stone and brick courthouse with a cupola and copper roof. The old courthouse, which had generated a community civil war, was torn down.

**Witnesses at Taylor County trials had better shine their shoes, as the witness chair, at left, doesn't hide them. Old mail slots are above. The courthouse dome, opposite page, is cleaned and polished every year.**

Taylor County

George Gale, who later became a judge, was one of Trempealeau County's early settlers. Gale, who lived in La Crosse, wanted to find an ideal location for a college. He bought 2,000 acres in the area that later became known as Galesville.

When Trempealeau County was created in 1854, Galesville seemed the most likely choice for the county seat. B.F. Heuston was elected county judge. Issac Noyes and Amassa P. Webb were awarded a $1,000 contract, plus $25 for materials, in 1855 to build a courthouse at Galesville. Lumber was hard to obtain and some was stolen from the courthouse site but the building opened in mid-1856.

Despite the influence of George Gale and the prestige of Gale

### Trempealeau County

**County seat: Whitehall**
**Current courthouse**
  **Year built: 1956**
  **Historic status: Not eligible due to insufficient age.**

The Trempealeau County Courthouse at Whitehall, circa 1910. Photo courtesy of State Historical Society of Wisconsin, ex. coll. John G. Gregory.

College, settlements in the Trempealeau Valley were growing faster than Galesville. In 1859, the people of Trempealeau Village petitioned to move the county seat to their community. Three years later, George F. Haswell of Buffalo County claimed that Trempealeau County was created illegally and he admonished Sheriff William A. Cramm for patrolling townships he claimed were in Buffalo County. The Wisconsin Supreme Court rejected the claim.

During the mid-1800s, transients boosted the local crime rate. "Strangers were constantly passing through the county and many of these travelers were of an unsavory character," Franklyn Curtiss-Wedge wrote in the *History of Trempealeau County.* "Unidentified bodies of murdered men were frequently found along the highways and corpses were often washing up at Trempealeau."

A new jail was authorized in 1867 and, a year later, a referendum failed to move the county seat to Trempealeau. By 1875, the first courthouse was in disrepair but efforts to spend $500 to fix it and to spend $5,000 on a new courthouse were defeated. Instead, voters decided in 1876 to move the county seat to Arcadia. A year later, Whitehall was approved in yet another referendum.

Arcadia residents weren't ready to give up. An 1882 referendum to move the county seat from Whitehall lost by a vote of 1,874-1,454. With the county seat question settled once and for all, a $20,000 courthouse was built in 1883 and an $8,000 jail was added three years later. In 1911, a courthouse addition and new jail were built.

The current courthouse was built in 1956 with additions in 1966 and 1976. The old courthouse was torn down for a new jail in 1983. A $3.8 million courthouse renovation project was completed in 1996.

Vernon County was organized as Bad Ax County in 1851 and the first court convened in Viroqua in a small log building erected the year before by Moses Decker.

**Vernon County**

County seat: Viroqua
**Current courthouse**
  **Year built: 1880**
  **Historic status: Listed in the National Register of Historic Places.**

In 1856, the first courthouse was torn down and a second courthouse, 30-feet by 38-feet, was built for $6,000. It housed six offices downstairs and a courtroom upstairs. Two years later, a jail was built for $2,060.

In 1880, Vernon County's current courthouse was built for $23,168. The 60-foot by 70-foot building includes a massive 42-foot by 58-foot courtroom.

A new jail was built in 1910 of red brick for $20,841. The jail included four cells for men, one for women and one for juveniles. A jail addition was built in 1974 and the jail was remodeled to house 27 inmates in 1990. A few years later, the historic courthouse was restored and rededicated.

One of the first cases involved a lawsuit by Daniel Lowry against Stephen Marston. The men were partners and when Marston noticed that Lowry was digging potatoes for personal use, he cut down all of the corn and took it home. Lowry sued and won a judgment against Marston from a justice of the peace but Marston appealed to circuit court. Lowry was represented by Royal C. Bierce while the attorney on the other side was William Terhune.

*Vernon County*

After hearing Terhune's arguments in the morning, Judge Knowlton recessed for lunch.

As Bierce began arguments against Lowry in the afternoon, Judge Knowlton settled back in his chair and ultimately fell asleep. Bierce continued to speak unruffled. When Bierce was finished, the judge awoke and retired to his chambers. Everyone awaited his decision but he didn't emerge for several days and finally people went home.

A few months later, the judge ruled against Terhune, leading to speculation about the eloquence of Bierce based on subliminal messages.

The only Vernon County lynching occurred June 1, 1888. A crowd of 200 angry citizens overpowered deputies, smashed open a cell door with a sledge hammer and dragged Andrew Grandstaff to a large tree in front of the courthouse, where they hung him. Grandstaff was accused of murdering a couple and their two grandchildren at Readstown. The hanging tree died after it was mutilated by collectors but a small stone in the courthouse marks the location.

**Murals brighten this Vernon County courtroom interior.**

Named for William F. Vilas, who served as U.S. Postmaster from 1885 to 1888, Vilas County had two towns, Eagle River and Minocqua, when it was created in 1893,

The first courthouse was completed in 1894 and the first jail was built two years later. In 1936, a new courthouse was built on the same site. By that time, the first courthouse was in dangerous condition so the county board appropriated $70,000 for a new building, although the lowest bid was $90,000. The first courthouse was torn down, but only four trees were removed and some 50-year-old trees were preserved.

The new courthouse was dedicated on Aug. 22, 1936, in conjunction with the county fair. In the cornerstone were placed board resolutions, a picture of the county board and copies of Time Magazine and the *Vilas County News-Review.*

An addition was built in 1976 and a new justice center was added in 1998.

### Vilas County

County seat: Eagle River
Current courthouse
  Year built: 1936
  Historic status: Not eligible due to insufficient age.

The Vilas County Courthouse in Eagle River, circa 1905. Photo courtesy of Ann Waidelich.

One of the most famous criminal cases in Vilas County was the shootout by federal agents with outlaw John Dillinger at Little Bohemia. Federal agents were criticized when they opened fire on a car leaving the resort. Inside the car were innocent civilians. Alerted by the gunfire, Dillinger managed to escape under return fire from his sidekick, George "Baby Face" Nelson. In 1935, the county board awarded compensation to Carl C. Christenson, who was wounded by federal agents.

**Vilas County**

# Walworth County

**The Walworth County Courthouse in Elkhorn, circa 1905. Photo courtesy of State Historical Society of Wisconsin.**

**Walworth County**

**County seat: Elkhorn**
**Current courthouse**
   **Year built: 1962**
   **Historic status: Not eligible due to insufficient age.**

Peace Nelson Campbell of the town of Geneva heard cases involving chicken thieves, horse traders, petty grievances and garnishments.

In 1962, Walworth County's fourth courthouse was built and the design received state and national recognition. President Kennedy had visited the previous courthouse and attended a county board meeting during his campaign.

A $19 million law enforcement center was proposed in 1995 but voters rejected several courthouse alternatives in a November 1996 referendum. Although the law enforcement center plan was endorsed by four circuit judges, the county board voted down the justice center in 1997 and the Elkhorn City Council proposed a $5.6 million addition instead.

Walworth County's first courthouse was built in 1839, one of the first in the state. The county was organized into five townships and Elkhorn was chosen as the county seat. Justice of the

The oldest settlement in Washburn county was the town of Veazie, headquarters of Walker, Judd and Veazie, one of the largest lumber companies of its era. The Veazie settlement was the center of social life for Washburn County and the last stop for supplies coming from Stillwater or St. Croix Falls.

During the latter part of the 19th Century, lumber drove the economy of Washburn County. The Shell Lake Lumber Co. was founded in 1880 and three years later the community was selected as the county seat when Washburn County was organized.

The first jail was constructed of two-by-six planks laid flat. The windows and doors had iron bars. Sheriffs William Beede and Pete Mills also had several ball-and-chain shackles for use when prisoners were assigned to work on road crews. Hoboes taken to jail for the night were given a hot breakfast, then taken out to work on a road gang to earn their keep.

Construction of the first courthouse began in 1889. A new courthouse was completed in 1989 and the old courthouse was torn down.

Shell Lake suffered two tragic fires. The first came on Dec. 3, 1889, and destroyed twenty businesses on Main Street. On Sept. 1, 1894, a forest fire swept into town and destroyed 60 homes on

**Washburn County**

County seat: **Shell Lake**
**Current courthouse**
Year built: **1989**
Historic status: **Not eligible due to loss of integrity.**

Bible Hill but the homes quickly were rebuilt. The fires may have symbolized the end of the white pine logging era as farming replaced the sawmills. The lumber company was dissolved in 1900 and the sawmill closed a year later. The once-important town of Veazie disappeared.

**The Washburn County Courthouse at Shell Lake, circa 1905. Photo courtesy of the State Historical Society of Wisconsin.**

**Washburn County**

## Washington County

The Washington County Courthouse's hilltop setting and towers create a castle-like appearance. Ironwork and a brightly patterned floor, opposite page, add warmth inside.

Washington County was created in 1853, when it was split off from Ozaukee County. With the split, however, Ozaukee County was too small so its boundaries were extended into Lake Michigan to get enough area.

When West Bend, then an unincorporated village of 500 people, was named the county seat, officials in Port Washington didn't want to move and also refused to surrender county records. After legal maneuvers were fruitless, a group from West Bend planned a clandestine raid to steal the records. The contingent broke into the register of deeds office in Port Washington and began stuffing documents in gunny sacks. But Port Washington officials had been tipped off to the raid and drove the raiders out of town. The records ultimately arrived in West Bend in a more legal manner.

In November 1853, the county board voted to change the name of West Bend to Lambertine City. But citizens quickly circulated a petition to change the name of Lambertine City back to West Bend. The petition was presented the next day and the board bowed to public pressure and changed the name back after West Bend had been Lambertine City for eighteen hours.

A frame courthouse, jail and jailer's residence

**Washington County**

County seat: West Bend
Historic courthouse
  Year built: 1889
  Historic status: Listed in the National Register of Historic Places.

in Greek Revival style were completed in 1854 and a fireproof one-story stone building for county offices was built three years later. The cost was $10,000. By 1883, the county buildings had become "monuments of disgrace," according to the *West Bend Democrat.*

In 1885, West Bend's population had grown to 1,300 and it was incorporated as a city. Edward V. Koch of Milwaukee designed a new jail which was used until 1967. Koch, who later designed the Milwaukee City Hall and courthouses in Door and Outagamie counties, was hired to design a new stone and brick courthouse, which was completed in 1889 for $45,000. The courthouse, one of the best examples of Romanesque Revival architecture, had terra cotta ornaments with a round arch and Gothic furnishings. It featured a tower and turrets at each corner. The courthouse, which was renovated in the 1960s for $2.4 million, also had red roofs and stained glass windows on the upper floor.

In 1899, the old frame courthouse was moved to Main and Hickory streets and became a hardware store. It was replaced with a building now known as the courthouse annex, which was built for $46,369.

In 1962, a new courthouse was built for $1.8 million. In 1980, a courthouse addition and law enforcement and corrections building were completed for $6.5 million.

# Washington County

Sunlight streams through stained glass windows, at left, in the courtroom interior. Below, the courthouse, now occupied by the historical society, is behind the old county jail.

The county's first courthouse, a two-story structure with a jury room and sheriff's office, was built in Greek Revival style for $10,000 in 1849. By 1892, the courthouse building was considered a fire hazard and architects Rau & Kirsch of Milwaukee submitted plans for a new courthouse.

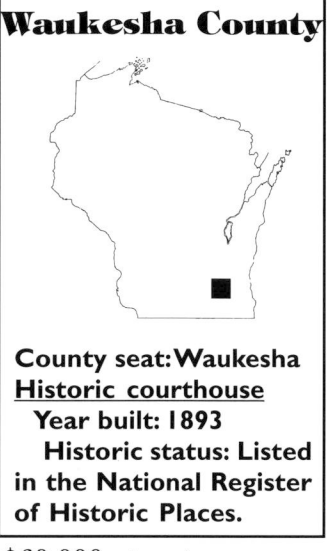

**Waukesha County**

County seat: Waukesha
**Historic courthouse**
Year built: 1893
Historic status: Listed in the National Register of Historic Places.

The original courthouse was demolished in 1893 and replaced by a $60,000 structure.

The second courthouse, which stood 130 feet tall, was built in Richardson Romanesque style with large archways and a castle-like appearance. It was constructed of polished granite quarried in Wisconsin with walls three feet thick. A seven-foot clock face was a hundred feet from the ground and the goddess of justice was placed on top.

With golden oak woodwork and an exterior of lannon stone, the courthouse featured a stained-glass window with an image of Christopher Columbus, significant because the courthouse was built during the year of Columbian Exposition, the world's fair that year in Chicago. Built on a turtle Indian mound, the courthouse's total cost was $69,100, including furnishings.

In 1905, a violent windstorm tore tiles from the courthouse roof. In 1950, the statue was taken down from the dome and regilded. A new courthouse was built in 1959 for $4 million. The statue was dam-

**A tall central tower and corner spires are prominent features of the old Waukesha County Courthouse.**

# Waukesha County

aged again in 1971 and, this time, it was removed and now stands on the second floor landing in the 1959 courthouse. A $17.2-million justice center was built in 1989. The second courthouse was preserved and is occupied by the Waukesha County Historical Society.

One of Waukesha County's most famous cases was the 1917 murder of Mary Newman Roberts by Grace Lusk. A spinster school teacher, Lusk was in love with the other woman's husband, Dr. David Roberts. After spending eleven months in the loft, the top floor of the 1885 jail used for women, Lusk was sentenced to nineteen years in prison. She was pardoned in 1923 by Gov. John Blaine after serving five years of her sentence.

**A circular staircase and safe, at left. The stained-glass window, opposite page, is at the east entrance and reflects the 1893 date of construction. The courthouse now is occupied by the historical society.**

The county seat battle in Waupaca County may have been the worst in the state with dueling county boards representing the eastern and western areas of the county. During the 1850s, westerners refused to send election results to the alleged county seat on the eastern side.

Waupaca County was created in 1851 and the county's first courthouse was built the following year at Mukwa, on the eastern side. Western county residents marched *en masse* across the county to vote at Mukwa and Waupaca won a referendum on where to locate the county seat. In Mukwa, however, the county board ignored the election results and reaffirmed that Mukwa would remain the county seat.

James Smiley of Mukwa became the first county clerk. In 1854, Waupaca officials claimed they won another referendum establishing Waupaca as the county seat. Easterners, however, claimed the vote in their part of the county was 302-41 against moving to Waupaca.

Weyauwega got into the fray the following year, when western voters rejected that community as a county seat by a 1,020-75 vote. Easterners, however, said Weyauwega had won by a 753-65 vote and Weyauwega was declared the county seat in 1856.

The bitter struggle finally was re-

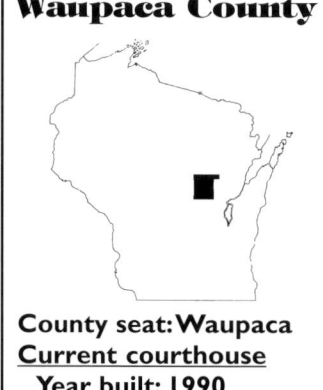

**Waupaca County**

County seat: Waupaca
Current courthouse
 Year built: 1990
 Historic status: Not eligible due to insufficient age.

solved in 1857 with an agreement that Smiley would no longer hold a county office. The Wisconsin Supreme Court ruled that Waupaca was the county seat and, in 1861, the first county board meeting was held there.

A jail was built in 1867 for $7,725 but the county had trouble building a courthouse due to old wounds from the county seat battle. A resolution to build a $12,000 courthouse was opposed by easterners in 1879. A $15,000 courthouse was built at Waupaca in 1890.

The courthouse was remodeled several times, including a 1906 addition, before it was sold to the city of Waupaca for $1 and later demolished. In 1990, a $10-million courthouse was completed.

The former Waupaca County Courthouse, circa 1905. Photo courtesy of State Historical Society of Wisconsin (postcard collection).

**Waushara County**

County seat: Wautoma
Current courthouse
Year built: 1929
Historic status: Listed in the National Register of Historic Places.

The county's 1888 courthouse lasted until April 30, 1928, when it burned to the ground. The only thing saved was a brick vault.

Later that year, the county board authorized $100,000 for a new courthouse but the final cost was $132,000 including furnishings. In 1978, a jail and courts addition were completed.

The first county judge was Thomas H. Walker, appointed in 1851. The first court was held the following year in Sacremento in the town

**Waushara County**

# Waushara County

of Aurora. In 1854, citizens voted to move the county seat to Wautoma.

An early murder case involved John Shontz and John Leahy. Shontz claimed a quarter of land in the town of Aurora but was unable to occupy it when he was stricken with fever in Illinois. Leahy and his wife took possession of the land and built a cabin on it.

When Shontz arrived, he threw out Leahy's wife and her belongings and tore down the cabin. Then he went to dinner. Returning later, he was confronted by Leahy and a gun.

"If you come close, I'll shoot," Leahy warned. Shontz dropped to one knee and fired a shotgun, killing Leahy. Schontz was acquitted of murder charges, claiming he acted in self-defense.

An old judge's bench, at left, now in the county board room. The statue above is a Civil War memorial.

**A winter's view of the historic Winnebago County Courthouse.**

Augustin Grignon was Winnebago County's first white settler, establishing a homestead at Butte des Morts in 1818.

When the county was created by the legislature about a quarter century later, somebody didn't study a map. The county seat was set at Manchester on the wrong side of Lake Winnebago in Calumet County. Settlers in Oshkosh refused to cross the lake and instead elected county officers at Webster Stanley's cabin, which in effect became the first courthouse.

Oshkosh, known by several names including Saukeer, Merton's Point, Stanley's Ferry, Knagg's Ferry and Athens, was designated the county seat in 1847 but residents of the older community of Butte des Morts demanded a referendum. In April 1850, voters rejected a proposal to move the county seat to Butte des Morts by a 690-472 vote.

An oak jail was quickly erected for $500 and a three-room office building was put up in 1853. In 1860, the county's first actual courthouse was completed for $19,689. Exterior walls of the two-story structure were of Milwaukee cream brick. The jail and sheriff's residence were in the basement.

Judge A.A. Austin was the county's first district attorney and served a total of 12 years in the office, although not consecutively. The first circuit judge was Alexander W. Stowe. Another district attorney, W.F. McArthur, was shot to death in 1883 while walking down a street in Neenah on his last day in office.

A new jail was built about the turn of the century for $15,000 and Winnebago County's latest courthouse was completed in 1938. The building features massive granite steps and symbolic carvings in limestone that frame a bronze doorway. Portuguese rose marble was used in the main lobby with gray French

**Winnebago County**

**County seat: Oshkosh**
**Current courthouse**
   **Year built: 1938**
   **Historic status: Listed in the National Register of Historic Places.**

marble in the corridors.

Two bronze lamp standards were placed at the main entrance and sculpting around the entrances was done by Alphonso Ianelli of Chicago. The sculptures were inspired by county historical events. The building's total cost was about $924,000.

The courthouse was rededicated in 1987 with a county coin developed for the occasion.

The trial of **Chief Oshkosh** is depicted by the mural above. On the opposite page are a courtroom interior, a bust of former President Reagan, commemorating a visit by Reagan to the courthouse, and carvings outside the courthouse.

**Winnebago County**

**Wood County**

County seat: Wisconsin Rapids
Current courthouse
  Year built: 1956
  Historic status: Not eligible due to insufficient age.

In 1866, a courthouse at Grand Rapids, later renamed Wisconsin Rapids, was built by Lyman Howe and John Rablin, along the river adjacent to the Grand Rapids Brewery. Most county officials, who were businessmen, continued to conduct their businesses from their own offices.

In 1872, the county board ordered the treasurer, register of deeds and other officials to move to the courthouse but the order had little effect. Only the sheriff had set up shop there.

The first courthouse had living quarters for the sheriff on the first floor and a jail in the basement. One inmate escaped by digging through the jail foundation but he was quickly recaptured two days later.

Despite a bitter fight that had broken out over which community should be the county seat, a new brick and stone courthouse was built at Grand Rapids in 1881 for $40,008. The old courthouse burned down in 1885.

In 1895, the county board decided to build a new jail and sheriff's residence. The State Board of Control threatened to condemn the jail, which had hosted many inmates despite poor ventilation and security.

The *Centralia Enterprise* reported: "Then, for the first time, it was discovered that the city of Grand Rapids, which had for more than 20 years had enjoyed the honor of being the seat of justice of Wood County, was in imminent danger that unless costly county buildings were at once erected... greenbackers might some day pick up the county seat, in the night, and carry it bodily away to some other point."

A $1-million courthouse and jail were completed in 1956. An addition was completed in 1976 and a larger jail added in 1987.

GREETINGS FROM GRAND RAPIDS, WIS.

The Wood County Courthouse, circa 1910. Photo courtesy of Ann Waidelich.

*Baraboo, Dells and Devil's Lake Region* by H.E. Cole, Baraboo News Publishing Co., Baraboo:1920.

*City in the Pinery* by Mary Anne Norton and Donald Aucutt, Marathon County Historical Society, 1984

*History of Buffalo and Pepin Counties,* compiled by Franklyn Curtiss-Wedge, H.C. Cooper Jr. & Co., Winona, Minn., 1919

"The Building on Our Square" by Tom Davis, *Wisconsin Trails,* November-December 1991

Stories in *Centralia Enterprise,* 1882

*Circuit Courth Visitors Guide,* various counties, Wisconsin Supreme Court/State Bar of Wisconsin, 1998

*Easy Going: Wisconsin's Northwoods, Vilas and Oneida counties* by Michael J. Dunn

*The Fat Memoirs* by Dave Engels

*Geneva Lake Area Intensive Survey: An Architectural/Historical Report,* pub. by Geneva Lake Land Conservancy and State Historical Society of Wisconsin, 1985.

*History of Grant County Wisconsin,* by Castello N. Holford, The Teller Print, Lancaster, Wis:1900

"New Courthouse in Grant County," *Milwaukee Free Press,* Aug. 29, 1902

*Grant County History 1900-1976,* pub. by the Resource Committee of Grant County

"Board Backs Court Funding," *Grant County Herald Independent,* March 20, 1997

*History of Iowa County,* Wisconsin, pub. by Western Historical Company, 1881

"L.A. Pradt, Lawyer, Dies at His Home From Heart Attack," *Wausau Daily Record Herald,* June 26, 1934

*Ladysmith Lore* by John M. Terrill, Richard Conklin and Sister Alice M. Henke.

*Law Day 1998: A History of Wisconsin's Courthouses,* Wisconsin Supreme Court, 1998

"Courts and the Legal Profession in Manitowoc County, Wisconsin: 1820 to the Present," by Edward Ehlert, Manitowoc County Historical Society, 1978

*A Souvenir of Marinette, Wisconsin,* pub. by C.O. Stiles, Iron Mountain, Mich.:1904

*Milwaukee County Circuit Court Visitors Guide,* published by Milwaukee Bar Association, 1997

"Decision Draws Near on Fate of Landmark," *Milwaukee Journal,* Jan. 7, 1968

"Reports to Menominees: Status of the County in the Legislature," by George Kenote, *Menominee Prints,* Oct. 13, 1969

*Monroe County, Wisconsin Heritage Book*

*The Oneida County Courthouse,* pamphlet

*History of Outagamie County, Wisconsin,* edited by Thomas H. Ryan, Goodspeed Historical Association, Chicago:1911

*Phillips, Wisconsin, 1876-1976*

*Polk County Place Names and Fact Book* by Ruth Bunker Christansen, 1976

*History of Portage County,* The Lewis Publishing Co., 1919

*Our County, Our Story: Portage County, Wisconsin* by Malcolm Rosholt, 1959

*Racine County Circuit Court Visitors Guide,* Racine County Bar Association, 1998

"Richland Ramblings: The Rose Zoldosky Casc," *Richland Observer,* Jan. 3, 1985-Feb. 14, 1985.

*Richland Center, Wisconsin: A History* by Margaret Helen Scott

"Parties and Politics in Rock County" by Charles A. Nelson, *Rock County Chronicle,* Spring 1960.

"Report of Judges for Janesville, Wisconsin," First Wisconsin Better Cities Contest, Wisconsin Conference of Social Work.

*Rock County Wisconsin* by William Fiske Brown, C.F. Cooper & Son, Chicago: 1908.

*History of the Saint Croix Valley* by Augustus B. Easton, H.C. Cooper & Co., 1909:Chicago

*St. Croix County Wisconsin,* by Eldora Schober Larson,Wisconsin Supreme County Sesquicentennial Project.

*The Shawano Story : 1874-1974* by Shawano Area Writers, Centennial Committee of the city of Shawano, Shawano:1974.

*A Short History of Southern Sawyer County* by W.Clark and M.H. Clark, The Wisconsin Colonization Co., Eau Claire.

*Landmarks: Sheboygan County Courthouse,* Sheboygan County Landmarks Ltd., 1934.

*Reminiscences and Anecdotes of Early Taylor County*

*History of Trempealeau County Wisconsin,* compiled by Franklyn Curtiss-Wedge, H.C. Cooper Jr. & Co. Chicago and Winona, 1917

*History of Vernon County,* 1884

*Historical Collections of Washburn County and the Surrounding Indianhead Country,* edit. by E. Ward Winton and Kay Brown Winton.

*Washington County Wisconsin: Past and Present,* edit. by Carl Quickert, S.J. Clarke Publishing Co., Chicago, 1912.

*Final Report: Intensive Architectural/Historical Survey of West Bend, Wisconsin* (1988)

*A Symbol of Truth and Law for Generations to Come: A Centennial History of Waukesha County's 1893 Courthouse*

*History of Waupaca County Wisconsin,* by J. Wakefield, pub. by D.L. Stinchfield of Waupaca, 1890

*Historical Sketch of Waushara County*

*History of Winnebago County Wisconsin: Its Cities, Towns, Resources, People,* by Publius V. Lawson, C.F. Cooper and Company, Chicago, 1908

"Wisconsin's Historic County Courthouses" by Rick Bernstein, *Wisconsin Counties,* April/August 1997

*History of Wood County Wisconsin,* 1923